CHRI

in KHOBAR

More Stories – Tim Barger

Al Khobar 1935

AL KHOBAR

In 1935 Al Khobar, located almost directly east of Bahrain Island, was a tiny fishing village on the coast of the Persian Gulf. Directly east about ten miles, the oil camp at Dhahran was just being established. Notice that there is no road, only a faint track, linking the village to the oil field. This would quickly change when the company built a modest pier at Khobar.

As Aramco grew, so did Khobar. Quite suddenly a few huts turned into a thriving town that became the commercial center of eastern Saudi Arabia. More than 70 years later it is still the heart of commerce on the eastern shores of the Gulf, but now it is a huge city, the anchor of a megalopolis stretching to Dhahran and north to Dammam.

For a great many Americans Khobar was their only contact with the energetic, culturally diversified society that flourished beyond the compound gates. Compared to the ordered, homogenized Aramco milieu, Khobar was a wild place populated with Saudi shopkeepers, Pakistani tailors, Yemeni laborers, Omani fishermen, Bedouin cab drivers, Syrian mechanics and a myriad of other nationalities all busily at work. Exotic women all clad in black drifting by.

Later in life, I was able to broaden my horizons to include Riyadh and Jeddah but my introduction to Saudi Arabia all started on the streets of Khobar in the 50s and I'll always be fond of the rich, cosmopolitan, laissez-faire attitude of its citizens. No one seemed to care about your race, religion or nationality; they just wanted to sell you something.

CHRISTMAS in KHOBAR

CHRISTMAS
in KHOBAR

More Stories – Tim Barger

Selwa Press

Copyright © 2017 Timothy J. Barger
ISBN: 978-0-9882050-1-7

Published by Selwa Press
Selwa Digital.com/ Selwa Press.com
Queries: Editor@SelwaPress.com

Cover: The author lighting a firecracker at Half Moon Bay
Back Cover photo by Dorothy Miller 1953
Book design by Ellen Goodwin

Table of Contents

DEDICATION

Dhahran -1951

To Tom and Kathleen for not
strangling me at birth
though on many occasions
it would have been perfectly justified.

Jebel Junibi at far right

IN MEMORIAM

To Jebel Midra Al-Junibi,
Generations of Saudis to come will
never know your beauty.

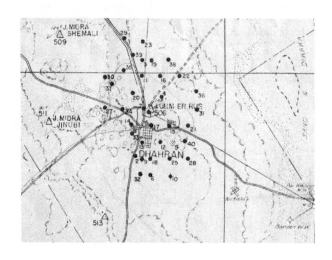

INTRODUCTION

This map pinpoints the locations of the first 40 wells drilled into the Dammam Dome, the geological name for the oil field that started everything in Saudi Arabia. It shows the Dhahran camp and the basic topography of the surrounding area to Al Khobar on the Gulf coast and toward the much older port of Dammam to the north.

To the west are the twin free-standing jebels: Jebel Midra Ash-Shemali at 509 feet tall and Jebel Midra Al-Junibi, which was two feet taller. Almost everything between these two landmarks and the Arabian Gulf is untouched desert, the same as it has always been.

In a stunning display of bad judgment, the governor of the Eastern Province delivered Jebel Junibi into the hands of a consortium of rapacious Saudi businessmen who leveled this 500-foot-high natural wonder to make cut limestone blocks.

The highest peak and one of the most unique micro-ecologies on the entire coast from Kuwait to Qatar, a specialized habitat replete with peculiar insects, rare plants, Neolithic markings, and a view to die for was reduced to bricks. I witnessed the last 30 feet of the jebel being methodically mined in 2012.

Today there isn't a piece of land east of Dhahran that is not developed. Homes, stores, apartment buildings, car lots, factories, stadiums, roads and freeways, offices and luxury malls cover the earth. There isn't any desert anymore.

Gone too are the herds of sprightly gazelle trotting through the morning mist, the jackals slinking around in the rocks, the hedgehogs and small foxes snug in their burrows, the huge lizards called *dhubb*s streaking across the sand.

Look up into the night sky, and you can barely see a star for the glare of the metropolis. The air smells of asphalt and exhaust. No matter where you turn there is no quiet. The quiet that is the voice of the desert.

It was almost an accident that 14 years ago I started writing these stories of my early life in Dhahran, and now there are almost forty. Twenty-one stories were included in my first collection *Arabian Son*, and here are some more.

It's a funny thing writing about the past. Do it enough, and you'll be transported there. You'll be eight years old, walking the shoreline of Half Moon Bay looking for beached sea snakes or drifting around in Khobar searching for comic books. You'll be seventeen, tending bar for Lou Reed and thirty wild teenagers in a Dhahran living room. The time that the MEA airliner's engine caught on fire, and we had to turn back to Beirut was interesting, too.

It was only recently, as I was writing "Center of Gravity," did I actually realize that I'm just shy of 70 years old. The adults I knew as a boy have long ago passed away, and the places I knew have been irrevocably changed or vanished all together.

There is nothing I can do to alter this, but I can tell you about a kid growing up in a 1950s oil camp in the Arabian desert, about floating, suspended in darkness, in an ancient well 40 feet beneath the Qatif oasis, about a pellet gun duel at sunset on the rocky slopes of Jebel Shamaal. I can immerse you in the fantastic chaos of the Used Car Suq in the Boomtown of 1974 Riyadh, or I can take you to the pristine shore of Half Moon Bay to watch a Viking funeral on the dark, placid water beneath a starry sky.

Tim Barger - 2017

A drilling rig in the Abqaiq field
- *Nestor Sander 1949*

CLARK RANDALL'S BIG BREAK

I'll call him Clark Randall. At 18, he volunteered for the Army. In early 1945, he went through basic training and was sent to Ft. Ord in Monterey to be trained as a diesel mechanic. He barely finished his training before the war ended, and he was mustered out. Clark returned home to Bakersfield and got a job in the nearby Taft oil field as an all-around field hand - mechanic, roughneck and rigger, working for Chevron. He became known as an energetic, young man with a secure, though not especially lucrative, future. A year later he married Jo Ellen, his high school sweetheart, and baby Bob showed up nine months later.

Clark did a lot of things well, but he was mechanically curious and always ready to learn some new aspect of the oil business, so his boss was glad to assign him to the non-routine jobs that spring up in the field. Replace a boiler, repair a section of pipeline, troubleshoot the pump at #17. Clark worked in Taft for three years but there were many older, more experienced men ahead of him, and there wasn't much room for advancement, so he started looking for something better.

About 1948, Chevron sold one of its surplus rigs to Aramco. The company was desperate to get as many rigs in action as it could, as fast as possible. Clark's boss put him in charge of breaking down one of these rigs and shipping it to Saudi Arabia. Clark considered the task, looked at the plant and the derrick, found an engineering drawing of the structure, numbered it up into sections and sub-sections, and then marked each piece accordingly with yellow paint as the crew disassembled the rig. Once everything was packed up, he delivered the annotated diagram and the detailed manifest of each crate and the parts it contained.

Clark had never considered Chevron's Arabian venture before, but a seed was planted. He asked around and was quickly hired by Aramco. Not much later he arrived in Abqaiq on a single-status contract for a provisional year before his family could come over. In 1949 things were hopping in the Abqaiq field but, when he arrived, as happened often, the personnel people weren't exactly sure where to put him, so he rotated from job to job as a substitute for some sick rigger or a mechanic on short leave.

This wasn't bad work, but it wasn't getting Clark anywhere as a career. As he missed Jo Ellen and Bob, he began to consider calling it quits after his year was up. One day between assignments, he was in his supervisor's office, and the man was telling him that they had received a rig shipped from the States. It had been mistakenly offloaded at Karachi but had finally arrived — only accompanied by the bills of lading; all the other documentation was missing. They had cabled San Francisco for instructions, but would Clark run down to Dhahran and check it out?

Leaving Abqaiq in his Dodge Power Wagon, Clark speculated about this errant shipment. But by the time he passed the decrepit cement-block halfway house on the two-lane blacktop road to Dhahran, it was so hot that he began anticipating a cold beer at the Stag Club when he finished this chore. It was a time when such a thing was legal within camp.

He introduced himself to Fritz, the manager of the breakout yard in Dhahran. They had a cup of coffee, talked shop, and enjoyed the AC for a few minutes. Fritz, an old-time bachelor, was enthusiastic about the AramcoCade, a sort of Esther Williams-inspired aquacade, that was going to be staged at the Dhahran Pool. He had visions of mermaids swimming before his eyes.

Fritz called in his right hand man, Hamood Ali, a short, wiry Qatifi with perfect posture and well-used laugh lines around his eyes. Clark liked him right away and followed him out of the office to find the shipment.

At the time Aramco had a small fleet of three-wheeled Italian motorcycles called Apes. Hamood hopped on his Ape, popped the clutch, and led Clark on a wild chase though the vast maze of the yard. They drove past lanes of stacked pipe, great bundles of rebar, huge wooden spools of wire, and then Clark followed Hamood around a corner and screeched to a halt. There was his rig. In his crates. Marked Taft, California. Clark was stunned. And then, in a stroke of divine inspiration, decided not to tell anyone what he knew. He and Hamood opened some of the crates with a crow bar. Clark grinned to himself as he recognized his own code numbers painted in yellow. After a while he drove back to Abqaiq.

"All the parts are there, and they are in good condition. Tell me where to put it up, give me a crew, and it'll be ready in a month," said Clark. His boss, who had dozens of new problems every day, looked at him and said, "Are you kidding me? It'll take that long to get the paperwork from the States."

"Everything is there. The rest is geometry. I've worked on rigs like this one, repaired parts of them. I'll work up a diagram, and we'll put it together. No problem. In a month."

The boss, whose mind was on the enormous Kenworth truck that had just rolled over with a load of pipe somewhere around Shedgum, paused to stare at Clark and finally said, "Okay. You got it. But screw this up, and you'll be drilling water wells in Qatif."

"I would insist on nothing less," said Clark.

Eventually the crates and pieces were delivered to somewhere in the desert south of Abqaiq. Five weeks later the rig was ready to go. Clark was golden, and he never looked back. It wasn't long before Jo Ellen and Bob joined him. Baby Fred came along a while later. After an illustrious career of more than twenty-five years, Clark retired as one of the most respected drilling operations supervisors in the Aramco oil patch.

New Houses in Abqaiq – 1949

WAJID ZAIN MEANS VERY GOOD

Martha was a housewife in Abqaiq (Ab-cake) in its earliest days – 1950 or so. Her husband was one of the best, if not the best, driller that ever operated out of Abqaiq. He was in the desert making Aramco rich, and she was in their house newly built on a patch of desert scraped flat with a bulldozer. Unimpeded by trees, a fence, or even blades of grass, the wind blew steady and whistled on as she sat in the dining room doing a jigsaw puzzle.

There is a faint tapping at the back door. Who could that be? At two in the afternoon? There is some more tapping, and she goes through the kitchen to the back door. About five feet from the bottom steps is an old man, grinning through a gold tooth and not many more. The hot wind catches his threadbare *guttra* to veil and unveil his well-worn face.

Martha knows the Pearl man, who limps from door to door with his Prussian blue velvet pouch of natural Gulf beauties – glowing opalescent spheres the size of lizard eggs, displayed to full effect against the dark blue cloth of his bag. The Shrimp man shows up occasionally with a burlap bag of shrimp packed in what looked like Aramco-issue ice – the kind with the hole through the middle. So his cousin works at the ice plant. But this old man is new.

Martha goes to the door and opens it to look at him standing there with an ancient, battered, wooden camel bowl in his hand. He says, "*Mimsahib. Wajid zain.*" And proffers the bowl toward her with a big mostly toothless smile.

It's so bright outside that it is hard to see much of anything. She opens the screen door and steps into her barren backyard as a momentary gust of wind obfuscates the old man in dust. She can't see what he is offering and says, "What?"

The old man brightens, takes a step forward and shows her the bowl. It contains some round dark things that definitely aren't pearls.

"What in the world is this?"

"*Mimsahib. Wajid zain,*" he says as he brings the bowl right close to Martha's face. "*Wajid zain. Wajid zain* shit."

He was selling fertilizer. The next weekend Aramco's foremost driller was tilling a couple of hundred pounds of *wajid zain*-grade goat pellets into his yard.

As told to me by a wonderful Abqaiq mother who arrived there at age 24 in 1950 and stayed for nearly thirty years.

Well fire at #12 – *Les Snyder 1939*

JOHN AMES

On May 1st 1939 King Abdul Aziz Ibn Saud inaugurated the first tanker load of Saudi oil at Ras Tanura, two months later the well being drilled at Dammam #12 exploded into a blazing inferno killing five Americans and Saudis.

Burning eight thousand barrels of oil a day, the well was lost but if the blowout continued the whole field was threatened because it might lose reservoir pressure so that the oil would have to be pumped out at great expense. With no outside expertise or fire-fighting equipment available for at least a month the oil men, resourceful veterans of overseas oil camps from Venezuela to Borneo, decided to extinguish the fire themselves.

At the time there was an eight-inch oil pipeline that went to Al-Khobar on the coast to fill oil barges bound for the BAPCO refinery in Bahrain. They flushed the pipe and reversed its flow to pump an inexhaustible flow of salt water to cool the flames. This whole episode is described by Wallace Stegner, the master author of the American West, in his book *Discovery: The Search for Arabian Oil.*

If you are able to watch the video of the disaster (it's available at Selwavideo on YouTube) you will easily understand the terrible conditions the oil men faced. It's July in Dhahran, so the daytime temperature is already 120 degrees, and the conflagration makes it even hotter. You can see the men working the hoses as they approach the fire, and then the wind shifts to push the men back with an invisible wall of unbearable heat. When the wind stops they move forward again.

Dozens of men are working the firehose but notice the two men at the nozzle. Wearing no protective clothing except gloves, the American in a felt hat and the Saudi in a *guttra*, maybe soaked in water, lead the attack on the flames. They are both there voluntarily. Fighting together against a common enemy that equally threatens their livelihood.

After ten days of battling the hellish flame that roared day and night like an out-of-control jet engine, on the afternoon of the 18th of July, when the temperature was already more than 110 degrees, Bill Eltiste, a tall, lanky engineer dressed in an asbestos suit, crouched behind a large steel shield on wheels that he slowly pushed toward the raging blowout as the air got hotter and hotter with every step. Around his waist was a thick cable to drag him back from the fire if he was overcome with heat.

Looking through a thin slit in the shield, Bill directed the bulldozer driver right behind him. He also wore an asbestos suit as he maneuvered a thirty-foot-long boom that held a sixty-foot-long pipe with a large funnel-shaped steel cone at the end. Water jets pounded the fire, and a thick spray doused the two men as they inched closer and closer to the unbearable heat. Using hand signals Eltiste guided the boom operator until, with his gloves smoldering, he dipped his fist, and the funnel dropped to snuff out the roaring torch. Suddenly it was quiet. The man driving the Caterpillar was John Ames, and when I was a kid, he lived next door to me.

John could operate any piece of heavy equipment from a bulldozer to a steam shovel with the same delicate touch; he could make just about anything with an arc welder, a cutting torch, and a stack of sheet steel. John was the kind of all-around guy that was the life-blood of an oil camp. Pragmatic, practical, versatile, and most importantly, good humored, he was one of the hundred Americans that remained in Dhahran during the war. Working seven days a week for five years, they pumped up to 10,000 barrels a day to Bahrain to top off the refinery and refuel the British navy in the struggle against Hitler.

John Ames at Manifa - 1941

In late November of 1942, John and Steve Furman went on a hunting trip in the Northern desert to bag some *hubbarah*, a large game bird, to be the turkeys for a somber Thanksgiving for these men isolated in a remote desert as the greatest war in history engulfed the world. They relished the feast, outdoing each other to make jokes and laugh and be in the spirit of the day, but behind his mask of easy camaraderie each man was thinking about his family: his wife, his children, brothers and sisters, aunts and uncles, his parents, cousins, nieces and nephews — and the damage this war would bring into their lives. There was not one thing he could do about it, but he could pump oil. So maybe it was time to tell the guys the story about when Lem Dawkins got his foot run over by Skinny Blake's pickup truck.

Nearly twenty years later, John had gained a few comfortable pounds but still sported his signature brush-top haircut, close cropped along the sidewalls like a Marine. His house was next to ours on 11th Street. As a young kid I'd sort of hover around peering through the fence made with *jareed* sticks of split-palm fronds tied together with a rust-colored jute string. He had converted his carport into a garage, and I would watch him use his torch to cut steel, braze things together, heat metal to a glow, and shape it with repeated blows of a big hammer against an anvil made from a piece of a cut-off railroad track.

Every once in a while he would glance at me and then quickly avert his eyes as if the point of the process was that I didn't exist, which was fine with me. Big, blustery friends of his would show up smoking, joking, and laughing, speaking an earthy language that immediately updated my mental thesaurus of four-letter words and colorful adjectives. It was the beginning of my career as an amateur lexicographer. Occasionally he'd be bantering with his pals and crack a slight smile to the kid behind the fence.

John was married to Esther — Esther Ames, MD. As the only American woman doctor in Aramco she spent a fair amount of time in Riyadh tending to the women of the royal family: the dowagers, the princesses, and their daughters. She was a great favorite and was showered with elaborate, hand-embroidered dresses, finely worked brass coffee pots, silk scarves, and the like. Sometimes Emir Saud bin Jiluwi, the governor and most powerful man in eastern Saudi Arabia, would send his personal black Cadillac and two bodyguards to take her to his palace.

John even managed to get a blade out of the connection when some grateful prince sent him a curved, eight-inch dagger with a jet-black onyx handle in a scabbard filigreed in fine gold-plated wire. He showed it to me once, and naturally I was completely impressed. However at the time, I knew none of this background. Only that at my parents' parties, John and Esther were having just as much fun as anybody else.

I'm almost ten and basically fanatical about snorkeling, fishing, Half Moon Bay, and gladiator movies. I had seen the now-classic Fall of Rome movie epic *Quo Vadis* three times. There was a bunch of dialogue about religion and some boring romantic stuff, but it featured the burning of Rome by Nero and some spectacular scenes of gladiators dueling in the Coliseum. They fought with fists, swords, clubs, and spears, but I was enthralled by the tall Nubian who fought with a net and a trident. He'd snare a giant, hairy Gaul frothing at the mouth with swords in both hands, yank him off his feet, and it was game over. Later in life I'd notice that the trident warrior would be in every gladiator movie, most especially Woody Strode's role in *Spartacus*. I also figured out that almost no one was as enthusiastic about gladiator movies as I was, and they would tend to shun me when I brought up the subject. They still do.

Leaving *Quo Vadis* I was convinced that if I had a trident spear I could easily gig dozens of those guppies that swarmed the shoreline of Half Moon Bay. I wasn't exactly a marine biologist and was totally ignorant about seafood, but my dad and his fishing pals would eat sardines out of a can while we drifted over the third reef, lines baited for *hamoor.* The guppies looked like sardines. A no-brainer: they'd go ape to eat fresh sardines. This is a good example of how faulty information can lead to flawed conclusions.

John used to hire me to sweep up his garage for a riyal, though I would have done it for free just to hang around. A few days after *Quo Vadis* he asked me to come over on Thursday morning. This was my big chance. I spent hours drawing the trident of my dreams. After many design changes I settled on a five-inch long point flanked by three-inch sub-spears.

After breakfast I folded the drawing into my back pocket and happened to find a broom that I was sure that nobody would miss and went into the backyard and sawed off the broom part. I failed to notice that there weren't any other brooms in the broom closet, just mops. This oversight would later be sharply corrected by higher authorities.

When I arrived, John with torch in hand was gently heating quarter-inch copper pipe from a big spool and wrapping it around a length of six-inch steel pipe. "Hi, Mr. Ames. What are you making?"

"Tim, I'm making a coil of copper pipe. When I'm finished it will be three feet high."

Why anyone would do that was beyond me, though later on I would understand the necessity for such a piece of sculpture. It was what they called a condenser, the cooling coil of a still. "You want me to start sweeping?"

He showed me where to start and went back to his spiral of copper. After a while he sawed off his creation from the spool, filed the edge, and released the copper coil to hold it up. "What do you think?"

The copper was fresh and shiny, and it was perfectly symmetrical. He softly pressed it down and let it rise up and down like a spring. He was grinning. "Mr. Ames, that's really wicked." It took him a second to understand that was a compliment, and then I made my pitch.

I told him about the Net Man in *Quo Vadis*, practically recreated the entire scene. And then told him my plan to harvest sardines at the beach. I thought he was smiling slightly, but he was probably trying to contain his hysterical laughter at the thought of my dad and Tom Handzus opening a sardine can full of guppies at the third reef.

I whipped out my drawing and showed him my idea of the perfect trident. He examined it carefully and said, "Are you sure this is what you want?"

"Oh yes, this is exactly like the movie, but I changed it a little and made it smaller." And then to clinch the deal I went over to the *jareed* fence and pulled out the broomstick I had wedged between the fronds. "I already have the shaft for the trident."

He said, "I can do that." He made me wear dark welder goggles as a yard away he cut the spearhead out of thin sheet-steel and brazed it to a short length of pipe the diameter of my broom stick. I pulled the goggles off and watched him work the tines with a grinder, sparks flying everywhere. He finished up, attached the head to the broom handle and handed me an actual replica of Poseidon's spear – or so I thought.

When I hit the beach at Half Moon Bay, I streaked to the shoreline and started spearing the first flock of guppies I saw. Except that the tines were too big and too far apart, and the guppies easily eluded me time after time. I finally figured that I should go deeper after the bigger fish. A ten-inch silver fish streaked before me in about four feet of water. I hurled the spear with stunning accuracy; unfortunately, the broom handle was extremely buoyant. The cunning weapon plunged in about three feet before the shaft popped straight back into my forehead. Oh well, it wasn't a perfect idea, but the trident held a special place of honor in the corner of my bedroom for years to come.

A few months later John came out of our house while I was messing around in the front yard and said, "Hey Tim.

I just talked to your dad, and he said it was okay for you to go shooting with me."

Shooting! I was a post-war kid raised on war movies and westerns. I had only shot my dad's .22 rifle when we spent long leave at my grandfather's ranch in North Dakota. "That'd be so wicked."

"Meet me in five minutes at my truck." I rushed into the house, thanked my dad, my mom, and my bewildered sister Mary as I hurried to my room to get my army surplus canteen, scurried to the kitchen to fill it, and ran out to the Dodge Power Wagon.

John came out with a US Army green canvas duffel bag rolled up lengthwise and placed it in the back of the truck, and we headed out of camp towards the junction of the Ras Tanura to Abqaiq road. We hung a left towards Abqaiq and the old Half Moon Bay entrance, drove on for a few miles before John pulled across the highway into the desert and headed for a ridge about half a mile off, between Dhahran and the road. He drove up to its base, and we hiked up to the top with the duffel bag over John's shoulder. He stopped to show me some jackal footprints in the sand.

The crest was fractured with slabs of broken rock interspersed with long drifts of sand. I took a long pull from my canteen and watched a truck travelling over the far-away asphalt. Jebel Shamaal loomed on the horizon north of us. John looked around, opened the duffel bag, and pulled out an M-1 Garand rifle. This was the real thing. The rifle used by American soldiers throughout the war. I started to hear the soundtrack from an Audie Murphy movie in my head. *The Sands of Iwo Jima* with John Wayne invaded my imagination.

"This is an M-1 rifle. If the enemy paratroopers were coming in from the west headed to Dhahran, where on this ridge would you shoot at them?" He had me from the moment I saw the rifle, but I managed to point at a cleft between two giant pieces of limestone.

"Good choice, Tim. It would be hard to get you there, but even a near miss would shower you with sharp rock fragments like a hundred tiny bullets. Over there on the sand crest is the place to go. Keep your head down, and when they shoot back at you the bullets will either miss or be absorbed in the sand. Here, I'll show you."

We went over to the sand, and he showed me how the rifle worked; he cycled the bolt action a few times, inserted the clip, went prone, and aimed the gun. "See, there is a black rock the size of a basketball down there about fifty yards away. That is the enemy."

I didn't really know who the enemy was supposed to be but innately understood that they were some Nazi scourge I had seen in countless movies and deserved a round in the basketball. John took careful aim, inhaled then exhaled, and squeezed off the first round. It sounded like thunder breaking six inches from my eardrum, echoing back at us as a puff of dust erupted from the black boulder. I almost missed the sound of the spent cartridge as it pinged back into the rocks.

It was one of those moments. The setting sun was starting to throw shadows on the terrain beneath us: a small canyon backed by another rocky ridge. John's hair was grayish white with age; his brush-top glistened in the golden light like the comb of some exotic Mohican raptor. His big pale-blue eyes peered out from his craggy face, gazing at the target for a minute before he lowered the weapon, turned to me with a crooked smile, said, "Watch this!" and settled into position.

He took a deep breath, let it out, and fired – and fired. He dissolved into a focused state that would have been welcomed from Bunker Hill to Omaha Beach. He emptied the clip in twenty seconds as the black rock spurted dust and rock chips with every hit. Heavy equipment wasn't the only kind of machinery he could operate.

Now it was my turn. He loaded another clip and handed the rifle to me as I stretched out in the sand. I couldn't quite get my shoulder to the rifle butt and still reach the trigger, so he steadied the back of the M-1 while I aimed it. I jerked the trigger on the first shot and missed by yards. A terrible shot but it didn't really matter. I had fired an M-1 rifle, which was one of the wildest dreams of almost every nine-year-old American boy born in the wake of World War II.

John taught me to keep the gun perfectly vertical and gently squeeze the trigger, and by my last shot I grazed the edge of the basketball, rewarded with a cloud of sand and rock splinters. He put in another clip and fired three rounds on one knee. Then he fired standing up. His last shot missed the rock. John paused and said, "Well, I guess I hit the Nazi next to him." He laughed, and we went back to Dhahran.

It wasn't until many years later did I learn that in the dark days of 1942 when Rommel had taken Tobruk and the Afrika Corps was rolling towards Cairo, the Americans had organized a contingency plan should German storm troopers try to seize the oil field. Some of the men would hold off the invaders long enough for the drillers to destroy the very wells they had so patiently drilled, and then everyone would flee south to the Emirates and from there to India. I don't know where the M-1 rifles came from, but a witness at the VJ Day – Victory in Japan day — celebrations in Dhahran on September 2, 1945 was amazed at the sheer amount of rifles and shotguns that magically appeared on King's Road to fire salvos into the air.

Seeing the present-day metropolis that stretches unbroken to Al-Khobar, it is easy to forget that seventy-five years ago Dhahran was a miniscule oil camp built on a desolate desert plateau by a thousand Saudis and a couple hundred Americans. Men who sweated in hundred-degree heat, pervasive humidity, and blinding sand storms to build an oil field out of nothing, who risked themselves to save it from a runaway well fire and were perfectly willing to fight to the end to prevent the Axis powers from capturing their wells intact.

They were professionals. Sure, they were paid well, but really they worked out of pride for their craft and the respect of their peers. Their greatest delight was problem-solving. Present the challenge, and they would get the job done, no matter what it took. They were men like my neighbor John Ames.

Al Khobar's main street with arches for King Saud's visit
– *Willard Drumm 1954*

CHRISTMAS in KHOBAR

I'm about eight and have ten riyals to buy Christmas presents for my family. No problem. The morning of Christmas Eve, I go to the canteen next to the mail center in the holiday spirit. The canteen is designed for bachelors who don't have time for the commissary and stocks the basics: khaki pants and shirts, hats, gloves, socks and underwear by the six-pack, razor blades, toothpaste, aspirin and nail clippers. Not the most exciting retail experience. However, near the front of the store behind a glass display case, adjacent to a huge assortment of cigars, is the most

fabulous selection of gum and candy bars south of Beirut —
at least to my stunted imagination.

The perfect place for present-buying. An O'Henry bar
for my older sister Annie, a Mars bar for my brother Mike,
a roll of Life Savers for my four-year-old sister Mary, and a
pack of Black Jack gum for my sister Norah who is two — I
had heard that she was having trouble with her gums. I give
my money to the clerk and am surprised to find out that I
now have only six riyals left. I was sure that Black Jack was
only half a riyal. I still haven't bought a present for my mom
and dad.

There is only one solution. I drift over to the front of
the Dining Hall and catch the bus. Somehow an eight-year-
old kid riding by himself to Khobar is considered perfectly
normal, but just in case, I drift behind two housewives as if
I'm vaguely connected with them, get on the bus unnoticed,
and quietly slip off at our destination. I'm in heaven as I
walk down Prince Khalid Avenue. There is everything in the
world that you could ever want. Firecrackers, fancy diving
watches, model airplanes, bicycles, switchblades, cameras,
pellet guns, real stuffed-alligators, fishing rods, and rattraps.
There is one agency showroom that displays what I now
know were designer Italian high-heels opposite a gleaming
portable cement mixer. No merchant is fussy about his
product mix. Sledge hammers or counterfeit Ban-Lon shirts
are all the same at the bottom line.

Khobar in those days was the most cosmopolitan city in eastern Arabia. The Saudis seemed to be perfectly relaxed about Christmas, which they considered as an Eid holiday for Americans. They knew it was a celebration of the birth of Jesus; he was respected within the Koran, and it seemed like a reasonable thing for Christians to commemorate. The general public loved the strings of multi-colored lights festooned on the store fronts. The one thing that they couldn't really comprehend was, "How did the bearded, fat guy in a red outfit figure into this whole program?" It was an endless source of fascination.

Of course the merchants, like their counterparts in America, quickly learned just how lucrative the holidays could be, and the stores sold a variety of artificial Christmas trees in a bewildering array of colors from natural green to electric blue to shocking purple. Plastic wreaths, shiny glass ornaments, strings of bubble lights, tinsel, and angel hair by the bale. One store window displayed half a dozen carved wood Nativity crèches surrounded by plastic snowmen and reindeers. Better yet, these Americans were madly buying presents for each other. This is Khobar after all, and business is good.

It's an unseasonably hot day, and after wandering around for a while, I'm getting thirsty and remember that my mom and sisters would drop into the Green Flag Store and get a free Pepsi, so I walk in. The first thing about the place is that the AC is super-frosty. I don't know how they did it, but they had the best AC in Khobar. Especially in the reception room, a small *madjlis*, cold as a meat locker with a few chairs and a couch.

I'm met at the door by a lean middle-aged man with gray hair and, behind wire-rimmed glasses, eyes that seem to be delighted to see you. I'll call him Selim, the owner of the store. We introduce ourselves, and Selim says, "Would you like a Pepsi?" My eyes widen like shiny, silver riyals, and he guides me back to the reception room.

Now, you need to understand that the Green Flag sold stuff that absolutely no one would ever want to buy. Towels, perfume, sheets, lipstick, pots and pans, nylon stockings, sets of silverware, dishes and glasses, Waring blenders, and Waterford crystal. I can't figure out how they can stay in business, but I have Pepsi on my mind.

I walk into the hospitality suite room to see two bachelorettes drinking Miranda orange soda on a sofa. *Oh... oh*, I know the red-haired woman.

A month or so before. Milt and I are wandering around after dinner in some alley when he tells me that last week the teenagers had a Scavenger Hunt party. A what?

Apparently they would meet at someone's house, be paired into teams and sent out with a list of stuff to collect. They had two hours to scavenge and then come back. Whoever had the most stuff won. My first question is, "Won what?"

Milt replies, "A hamburger and milkshake at the Fiesta Room."

Not too shoddy, I think to myself. "And what did they have to collect?"

Milt says, "Mostly junk. A copy of *The Sun and Flare*, an old shoe, a sand dollar, an empty Pepsi bottle, a burnt-out light bulb, a broken fork, a matchbook from the States, a pipe cleaner - *A stick of Beeman's gum.*"

Spontaneously, we have a terrific idea. We rummage through the nearest garbage can and come up with a piece of brown paper bag, and Milt has one of those short pencils that are free at the golf course. Under a streetlight, I flatten the paper over my thigh and write up our list.

Skavenjer Hunt

1. Old newspaper
2. Shovel
3. Spear Gun
4. Pepsi
5. Another Pepsi
6. Firecrackers
7. Black Jack or any kind of gum
8. Cookies
9. Box of grape Jell-O
10. Golf ball

Since we didn't want them anyway, we cross out newspaper, shovel and golf ball – as if we already had them.

We hold out for the spear gun and head to the bachelorette portable situated on the broad median that intersected 11th Street as it flowed down to the AC plant. About six single women lived there. I ring the doorbell, and a red-haired lady — she was probably in her late twenties — opens the door. It is doom; she knows me. "Hi, Tim. How's your mother doing? Beautiful Norah probably keeps her busy." I later find out her name is Molly.

"Oh, she's fine. Though she burps a lot. Ah… I mean Norah does. We're on a scavenger hunt. Milt and I are supposed to get this stuff." And I hand her the scrawled list.

She scans it with a straight face, although she is probably dying of hysterics. Looking back, I really am grateful to her and the many other adults who cut me enough slack to not break into uncontrollable laughter on the spot. "We had a spear gun, but I think Skinny picked it up yesterday. I'll check," and, looking away for a second, says, "I think Sylvia lit off all of her firecrackers at the big dance at the patio last Thursday night." She pauses for a bemused moment, "But let me see what we've got."

Milt and I are shuffling around in the small reception room. Wondering if she is going to call our mothers, somehow check up on us. We're about to bolt into the night when Molly appears with her hands behind her back.

"Sorry, but the spear gun is gone. Aimee ate the last four cookies and chewed all the gum. But I do have these," and she brought forth two cold Pepsis and a box of Jell-O. Lime Jell-O, probably the worst flavor, but who is choosy?

We are effusive and completely obsequious as we back out of the portable and head off into the night. Except we have a problem. Three minutes later, I am back at the portable, knocking on the door. Molly answers, "Oh, hi, Tim."

"I forgot, but we're supposed to get a bottle opener, too."

The dear woman. I have no idea how she didn't collapse into convulsions. Anyway, she maintains a stiff upper lip about to shatter into giggling pieces and returns with a rusty church key.

We thank her and flee to the ample hedge surrounding the tennis courts. We worm into a favorite burrow within the vegetation, conveniently powdered in DDT, and pull out our stash. We eat big chunks of abused, year-old Jell-O that has congealed into a solid piece, then wash it down with swigs of Pepsi that make the Jell-O fizz up in our throats, and our blood sugar count soars into the Guinness Book of Records.

But now Molly and her friend are sitting on the sofa in the Green Flag store, and I am toast. "Hi, Tim. How's your mom doing? Is she here?" I'm speechless but, for the first time, notice her pale green eyes, her high cheekbones, and her slightly crooked smile. She might actually be attractive if she weren't so old.

I don't know what to respond, but fortunately, a tiny lawyer appears on my shoulder, and I say, "Molly. Oh, hi. She likes Balooki's." Another store that sold useless things like draperies, towels, pillows, bedspreads and washing machines.

"Oh, maybe I'll bump into her over there. If I miss her, please say hello for me."

"Sure, I'll tell her."

"Thanks. We still have some shopping to do. Good seeing you again." And the two women leave me sitting in a green suede easy-chair listening to the steady thrum of the dual AC window units, staring at the pale yellow wallpaper flocked with a purple spider web pattern. I am totally ignorant of interior design but wonder, *Where on the planet Mars did they find this paper?*

Selim comes in with a frosty Pepsi, hands it to me, and says, "Here, Mr. Tim, have a soda." He pauses a moment and says, "Do you mind if I join you?" The man just gave me a Pepsi; of course he can join me. For a moment, I stop drinking what is basically a huge dose of sugar and caffeine — Red Bull before its time — and tell him that it's my pleasure.

It's a weird fact that the formula for the Pepsi that the Al Gossaibi company bottled in Khobar contained twice as much sugar as an American Pepsi. Now the stuff is imported in cans, and that's why you'll never taste a real Arabian Pepsi again.

Anyway, Selim sits down in the other over-stuffed chair. He sort of disassembles himself, like a puppet who has relaxed all his strings. He closes his eyes and drifts. I'm perfectly happy drinking my soda, but I'm starting to grip about getting those presents. Time's running short. I'm going to have to get back to the bus. If I miss it and this trip to Khobar is discovered, my future movements will be severely restricted.

What I need to do is ask Selim. What should I say to him that would break the ice?

I sort of cough and then say, "Mr. Selim?"

His eyes blink open, he reconnects all of his ligaments, and says, "Yes, Mr. Tim. How are you?"

"Oh, I'm fine. I was just wondering where did you buy this wallpaper?"

Glee sweeps his face and he grins to say, "Last year, my brother Ali went to the trade fair in Hamburg, and he got... Waving his arms, "He got carried away."

Being diplomatic, I say, "I've never seen anything like this."

He laughs and says, "And I hope I never do again. Tell me, can I be of service?"

So I tell him about my dilemma. What to get for Mom and Dad. Tonight was Christmas Eve. I only had an hour left to catch the bus. I drained the last of the Pepsi to further jangle my nerves. Watching my parents in the *suq*, I knew that it was a special technique to not reveal how much money you had, so I cannily didn't mention that I only had six riyals and eight quirsh.

He says, "Maybe your mother would like some perfume?"

The best of the Khobar merchants have a preternatural ability to instantly diagnose any human who walks into their store. Triage the lookers, the maybes and the sure sale; then with a sort of X-ray vision determine to the riyal how much each one of them has in pocket. I'm sure that Selim pegged me for nine riyals, so I have the bargaining advantage. But Selim is no longer in it for the sale. He is just delighted that someone else has recognized that Ali is an idiot. He still has a pallet of that wallpaper turning into mildew in the warehouse.

I follow him back into the store, and he slips behind the perfume counter strategically placed next to a display of brooms, mops, feather dusters and toilet plungers arranged around an upright vacuum cleaner. He scans the shelves and selects a very small green bottle with a gold label. He dabs a bit on a stamp-sized square of paper and hands it to me. "This is a famous scent. I'm sure that your mother will enjoy it. It's made in Paris. It's called *4711*."

It smells good. Actually, it smells like Molly, and I think she has class – so it must be okay. "That smells great. How much does it cost?" Thinking it's such a small bottle it can't be more than three riyals.

"Twenty-five riyals."

What! I didn't ask to buy the store. "Ah… well, what else do you have?"

"Oh, let me see. Yes, this is very economical," as he pulls down a larger, purple bottle with a silver label. "It's called *Midnight in Port Said.* It's made in Cairo. It's only two riyals."

He hands me the sample, and I recoil at the classic scent of all those bottles of Air-Wick fuming through the bathrooms of Aramco. I don't even have to shake my head in disapproval. Selim seems pleased at my discriminating nose.

"Mr. Tim, I agree with you. Here, try this," and pulls out another bottle that is surprisingly similar to the first one – in fact almost identical. "This is a fine cologne from Bulgaria. It is called *1174.*"

It doesn't smell anywhere as good as the first sample, but maybe the price is right, "How much is this stuff?"

"Well, it's ten riyals, but for you… it's six."

My whole bank roll. But again I've seen enough bargaining to know I should counter, "Four riyals."

He gives me a doleful look and says, "Mr. Tim, I already made the price so small. If I sell it for less… I will have no food for my children when I go home tonight," and the laugh lines around his eyes betray his attempt to keep a straight face. "However, I could sell it to you for five riyals and have enough to maybe buy some bread for my family."

What do you know? Another adult trying to contain a spontaneous eruption of laughter. Though I don't notice because I really have to close this deal and scurry on, so shrewdly I make my final offer, "Four riyals and eight quirsh."

"I knew that you would see it my way. It's a deal." He shakes my hand, picks up the bottle and turns his back to me. "Here, I'll wrap it up for you." After a couple minutes he gives me a small box neatly wrapped in gold foil. I pay him, and he says, "Merry Christmas, Mr. Tim," as I walk out the door onto Prince Khalid Street.

Al-Khobar - *Dorothy Miller 1952*

Al-Khobar in the mid-fifties is a booming, fantastic place; an exotic contrast to the efficient conformity of camp, which has central water and air-conditioning but never the opportunity to see a Yemeni walking down the street with a baboon or brightly turbaned Persians selling pastel-colored canaries from woven cane cages.

The streets are alive with an astounding cast of characters. Predominantly Saudis from every station of life but intermingled with a broad sample of Arabs, Asians, and Africans drawn to opportunity. Egyptians, Indians, Sudanese, Iraqis, Pakistanis, Palestinians, Omanis, Somalis, and Bahrainis, punctuated with a sprinkling of Europeans and of course the only true foreigners, the inhabitants of the Western hemisphere – the Americans.

The city doesn't extend more than a quarter mile from the beach, and the coast is much nearer because there is no landfilled corniche as there is today. At the south end of town the famous Khobar pier extends into the Gulf. It is an intriguing place of sailing dhows and foul-smelling, diesel-powered motor launches populated by sailors, fishermen, and stevedores from all over the Gulf.

Just north, past a block or two of open parking ground for trucks, buses, and cars, begins the main street named after the then-Prince Khalid, later King Khalid. It's a lively strip, fronted with stores of every kind. If you are four feet tall, it is quite a spectacle, but I am in a hurry. I have to find a present for my dad, and I can't miss the bus.

Walking down the street, I notice a shop with a Grundig Multi-band Shortwave radio prominently displayed in the window surrounded by black telephones filigreed with gold paint like a Singer sewing machine. I go up to the glass. *Boy, would my dad like that. Yeah, sure. For about a million riyals.*

And I push on down the road.

I have a special weakness for a store near the middle of the street that has a window display of machetes, pocket knives, and switch blades. I stop to marvel at the weapons, especially the designs on the stilettos. You have to admit that the classic, black switchblade with a silver grinning skull on the handle is a definite crowd pleaser; however, I have my eye on a certain blade.

It has a bone-colored handle elaborately painted in red lacquer depicting some sort of devil squid with its tentacles grasping up to the sharp steel. And to the side in the back of the display is the *pièce de résistance*, an actual pair of brass knuckles. I don't know if they are sold as a set or individually, but I am certain that my dad would love to have some brass knuckles, in case he got into a dust-up. Unfortunately, I had priced them months before, and the prices are stratospheric. They want 12 riyals for the squid blade. Time to move on.

At the time Khobar, and its environs from Hofuf to Qatif, is not fully mechanized. A donkey cart with balloon tires is still very cost-competitive, especially compared to the price of a Ford truck. So the donkeys trot along with the Buicks, and once in a while some camels pass down the avenue. But those days are fading along with another phenomenon that hardly anyone remembers anymore. Up and down the street, at strategic locations on the sidewalk, old men sell cigarettes out of a sort of trunk on tiny wheels. They are very interesting.

Prince Khalid Street, Al-Khobar - *Dorothy Miller 1952*

Hanging around on the street waiting for my mom and sisters to finally leave the charm bracelet counter at Zain Jewelers, I would watch them at work. A customer would approach and pick up a pack of Camels. The absolutely indifferent codger would rummage around and produce an opened, but intact carton of Camels. He'd root around within the carton and produce a stamp, hand it to the customer who would pay his riyal and then hand the stamp back to the old man who'd replace the stamp in the intact carton.

My dad explained it to me at the time which I didn't fully understand, but basically they sold smuggled cigarettes. They had one legal carton of each brand with the prerequisite amount of loose tax stamps and then sold tons of untaxed smokes. Looking back now, what appeared to be haphazard locations along the boulevard where actually prime, jealously guarded sites. The vendors weren't especially friendly to kids – as if I was going to buy a carton of Lucky Strikes.

However, they also sold boxes of Binzager wooden matches, Chiclets made about the time of the Civil War, and lighters. That's it. I'll buy my dad a lighter. At the end of the street, near where the bus to Dhahran parks, I approach the cigarette man. He's selling a pack of Winstons to a Lebanese mechanic who doesn't have change for a hundred. While they're bickering, I scan the lighters. Cheap Zippo knock-offs in white enamel, silk-screened with a variety of designs: a rose, a Saudi Arabian flag, a race car, an F-86 Saber jet, some Bollywood temptress, the head of a German shepherd, and three portraits of King Saud. The pose in the middle speaks to me, and I just know that my dad will be thrilled to have this beautiful likeness of the king.

The cigarette man finishes with the Lebanese and spins to cast a rheumy eye my way. I point at the lighter. He grunts and holds up four fingers. I don't know how to say a riyal and a half, so I hold up two fingers. He's already pretty disgusted with me, but finally holds up three fingers. Well, I'm out of haggling tricks, so I lamely hold up two fingers again. He shakes his head and dismisses me with a sharp hiss. Defeated, I scamper off towards the bus and come to a dead halt. There is a complication.

Molly and her friend are approaching the bus. I can't let her see me solo. I'm stressing out when I notice a hapless Saudi teenager staggering behind them carrying a big, elaborate, throne-like, wicker chair. The women confer for a moment and then summon a taxi. The driver manages to cram the chair into the trunk, and they drive off. I make a beeline for the bus.

Riding back to Dhahran I'm running a critical path analysis in my head. I do have my mom's present, but once we get to camp I'll have to hit the company store again before it closes and find something for my dad. What could that be? I streak over to the canteen and desperately search for anything that costs two riyals. I can get him a pack of safety razors, a can of chewing tobacco, a bandanna in red or blue, a big dispenser of dental floss or... I find it! The clerk confirms that it costs two riyals. I seal the deal and rush home.

The house is bustling with activity, everyone getting ready for Christmas Eve, and no one notices as I slip into the kitchen, snag the tin foil and snake back into the bedroom that I share with my brother Michael who isn't there. Adroitly, or so I think, I rip off long jagged pieces of tin foil and wrap the candy bars and my dad's present. I can't find a pencil, so with a crayon I scrawl out the name tags on some index cards that I've torn into irregular pieces because I can't find any scissors either.

I tape the tags to the presents, wrap each one with some more masking tape for good measure, and I'm done. They look pretty sharp to me, but they actually resemble small, squished, baked potatoes wrapped in the remnants of a wrinkled hazmat suit, strangled in randomly applied strips of brown paper tape. I'm good to go.

The house is decked in candy canes and mistletoe. The fully decorated artificial tree that I had accidentally toppled to the ground ten days ago, when I tripped over the light cord, is back in place with maybe a fewer glass ball ornaments than planned, smothered in tinsel and angel hair. Our family tradition was to have Christmas Eve dinner with a few close friends such as my godparents, Steve and Claudine Furman, and maybe a grizzled, old-time bachelor or two at loose ends. Then open the presents.

Of course this dinner is absolute torture for all of us kids. Even my 14-year-old sister Annie is twitching around. Her heart is set on getting a fancy, new bridle for her horse Alia. My brother has his hopes pinned on a large-scale plastic model of a Corvette he spotted in Jameel's a month ago, and I'm torn between getting a periscope or a boomerang. Preferably both. Mary is probably dreaming about some *Betsy Wetsy* kind of doll or even her own cookie sheet. Norah is eating Gerber's banana pudding in the high chair, occasionally banging her spoon at inappropriate moments.

Except for Norah, we are all dying of anxiety as the adults drone on. Steve Furman has another helping of *hamoor*. The brilliant, gaunt geologist Dick Bramkamp pauses mid-meal to smoke a Pall Mall, which nobody even notices. My mom has some more waxed beans. The same completely inedible wax beans that I have cut into tiny pieces and artfully scattered around my plate, with the excess buried under the rice.

Finally dinner is over. Time for dessert. We are all on the same page as we devour our genius cook Nickie's splendid strawberry meringues. The strawberries topped with whipped cream are Bird's Eye frozen and defrosted, but the meringues are a Nickie specialty. They would equal the finest confection in Vienna. Everyone is amiable. There is peace on earth and all that, when my mother says, "Coffee, anyone?"

All of us kids, including Annie, groan; we know what this means. The adults sit around drinking coffee endlessly, smoking, laughing, and talking about people and subjects that we can't possibly comprehend. Then we hear more bad news: "More coffee, anyone?"

We can't take it anymore and slip away from the table to gather in the living room and fantasize about what each present might contain. I especially admire the wrapping job on my dad's present. The tin foil kept ripping unevenly, so I clumped hunks of the foil around the cylinder and cleverly wrapped it all in uneven, irregular strands of masking tape. It looks like a lumpy, pipe bomb made by a first grader with unresolved motor-skill issues.

Eventually, we start opening presents, one by one, starting at the youngest. Norah scores the first gift, which happens to be mine. Mary, with a great deal of effort — she even bites into the layers of masking tape — manages to unwrap the Black Jack gum and hands it, unopened, to Norah, who snatches up the entire pack, puts it in her mouth like some kind of weird pacifier and happily chomps away. And the present exchange is off and running. After each present everyone exclaims at what a great present it is, claps or whistles.

Eventually my mom holds up my gift, comments on how nicely it's wrapped, and says, "Oh Tim, what could this be?" She peels off the gold foil paper and says. "Timothy! How did you ever know that 4711 is my favorite cologne? What a beautiful Christmas present. Thank you."

I'm shocked. I lurch forward to give her a hug, but I'm desperate to get a closer look at the bottle. Wasn't it supposed to be 1174? You know, the perfume they make in Bulgaria. Sure enough, it's 4711, the real thing. I send up a heartfelt, silent thanks to the wily Mr. Selim.

It's a regrettable fact that we grow up, become adults and gradually lose an appreciation for the intense acuity that we had as children. For instance, when your dad is about to open your misshapen present, you shift into a sort of slow-motion scrutiny. What happens in five seconds seems to happen in a minute. First, he examines the dyslexic wrapping job, then he splits it open to view the prize. At this moment you have to watch for the tell, his expression when he first sees what it is. Unfortunately, though it only lasts for a millisecond, I can see that my dad is totally baffled. He recovers and says, "Tim, thanks. I can really use this." And then raises it up for everyone to see. There is total silence. He is holding up a tall, thin, glass bottle that contains 20 tablets of Alka-Seltzer.

Even my mom is speechless. Annie starts to giggle, but my godfather, Steve Furman, lets out a big laugh and says, "Tom, you'll need to get another bottle to survive my New Year's Day chili feast." Everyone laughs. My dad gives me a great hug, and the festivities continue.

More than 30 years later, my father has passed away, and I gather with my siblings at his house in coastal San Diego to perform that sad duty that most all of us will someday face: sorting through the family home, pulling down dozens of boxes and suitcases from the attic, getting side-tracked reading old letters, dividing up the personal items and framed pictures – each one a tangible echo of a specific memory that we had growing up. But it isn't all long faces. Every discovery elicits some kind of exclamation. "I got this Raggedy Ann doll for my birthday!" "These are Mom's spoons from her grandmother!" "Here's Dad's passport from 1937!"

At the end of the second day, we drift into the master bedroom, and I spread about 400 snapshots, spanning more than 60 years, on the bed. Clustered around the huge mattress, we spend hours looking at them. Photo by photo, everyone chipping in with their comments. Bantering, identifying places and family friends, laughing, sometimes crying. Walking each other down a sweet, sometimes bittersweet, lane of vivid memories.

I am in charge of processing my dad's office, which has a sliding glass door with a great view of the distant ocean. I curate his many books, separate the ten-year-old utility bills from his personal papers, and pitch the various gadgets that he had, to no avail, acquired to improve his golf game.

On the morning of the third day I'm tackling a tall four-drawer filing cabinet. I've finished the first drawer when I realize that there is some more room behind the files. I reach in and pull out a cigar box. My dad loved cigar boxes because they were sturdy, had a standard shape and were functionally air-tight – a vital consideration in Saudi Arabia's pervasive sand and humidity, especially in the 1940s before universal air-conditioning.

I place the box atop the cabinet and lift the lid. Covering the contents is an operating manual for some long-gone drill press. Beneath is a scratched and well-used, retractable, compact magnifying glass and a Brunton compass, the tools he used as a field geologist. Toward the back of the box is an empty, weathered envelope with a passport photo from about 1938 almost welded to the outside by a rusty paper clip. I pick up the envelope and uncover a still-sealed, thin, glass bottle containing 20 Alka-Seltzer tablets.

Stunned, I stare at it as if am looking into a crystal ball. After a few minutes, I put the cigar box aside on my dad's desk and display the Alka-Seltzer on one of the bookshelves. I go back to digging through the other three file drawers.

The place is a madhouse. We are all running around hauling out Hefty bags of old junk, shifting furniture, assembling cardboard boxes, bubble-wrapping anything that moves, on the phone to shipping companies, and the pile of stuff for the Disabled War Vets grows ever taller. Later in the day I return to the office to find that the Alka-Seltzer bottle is gone.

I look around, check the floor and then notice that the two overflowing waste baskets in the office are now empty. My sisters are energetic and conscientious beyond belief. I guess that one of them came into to collect the trash, spotted the Alka Seltzer bottle, checked the expiration date – 1955, decided that it was probably a toxic poison by now, and pitched it.

I think about digging through the trash, but there are more than a dozen bags of debris in the garage waiting for the curbside pickup in the morning. I can't really make an issue of the loss, or even mention it, as everyone is working so hard to pack up the house. Standing in my dad's study as the sun finally sets over the Pacific, I realize that the Alka-Seltzer doesn't really matter. It was only a message in a bottle. And I got the message.

County Fair Parade– *Les Snyder 1939*

CLICK!

Doug Strader was a lanky sixth grader who lived on the next block. Our families were close friends, so even though I was a fourth grader, if none of his peers were around, he'd mentor me on the finer points of sophisticated behavior.

This blazing, bright-hot afternoon, Doug and I are in the narrow lot along the concrete walkway between the library and the swimming pool, a space currently occupied by one of those big Swedish pre-fab buildings, which was used as a temporary classroom. I believe that this was the

portable that hosted the infamous event wherein Ralph
W. got clobbered by a falling light fixture. It's hard to say
because this particular building had fallen into some sort
of corporate Groundhog's Day, and Aramco was forever
moving it out and then, months later, bringing it back in.

On this particular day the portable was empty, up
on wooden shorings, and ready to be moved out. We are
hanging around in the shade of the library, staring at the
pre-fab. Doug is telling me how to get free into the movies
by sneaking through the exit door, when he snatches up a
rock and throws it through a window with a great crash and
the tinkle of falling glass.

My first impulse is to run like hell, but Doug says, "It's
okay. Aramco doesn't want this portable. They're gonna take
it to Reclamation and crush it. They want you to break the
windows."

"Me? What? How do you know?' I ask.

"My dad told me. It's true."

I think that this is too good to be true, but I'm happy to
believe it. I pick up a decent size rock.

Doug already has another stone and says, "Watch this!"
and pegs it through the glass window on the door. The
sound of breaking glass in the afternoon. What great fun —
and legal, too.

With my rock ready to throw, I rush up to the door and
am about to deliver my best knuckleball when I see Doug's

mother. She is standing behind the door, looking through the broken glass. I freeze and casually drop the rock behind my back, but she doesn't really see me because she is staring the Anger Ray of Death straight at Doug.

A small, feisty woman with a powerful voice, Mitzi Strader is screaming at Doug and then actually grabs his ear and drags him away, giving me a nasty look as she passes. To this day, I can never figure out how she happened to show up behind that window three seconds after Doug broke it. She must have seen us loitering around the building down at the other end of the walkway and went through the back door to check up on us. A mom's instinct for trouble proven once again to be entirely accurate.

Walking home, I'm considering my legal rights as explained by my law professor Perry Mason. I didn't actually break a window — though I sure was ready to— so I was in the clear. Fortunately, I'm blissfully unaware of the various statutes related to conspiracy and accomplices. I was about to learn that not guilty doesn't always mean innocent.

A couple of hours later, guiltless as a lamb, I'm in my room gluing the wings of a Japanese Mitsubishi Zero together. I was into those Aurora plastic models. I'm finished and pick up the two fuselage halves I'm going to glue next, when I hear my mother say, "Timothy!"

Of course, Mrs. Strader has called my mom, Kathleen. And now I'm literally on the carpet in the living room protesting my innocence. "I didn't break any windows. I was just watching. Doug said it was okay."

With a stern look, she says, "You shouldn't have even been there. But that's not what Mitzi told me."

"What? What did she say?"

"She said that Doug told her that you dared him to break the window."

"What…"

"I don't care what either of you say. You were hanging around like a couple of hoodlums looking for trouble."

"But… But…" I say, trying to come up with a quote from Perry, but she cuts me short.

"Timothy, you have to pay attention in life. You don't break windows. You don't damage other people's property. You don't even think about it. I'm really sorry because it's so much fun, but you can't go the fair tomorrow. You're staying home."

A chill splits my spine; my vertebrae tingle with fear. "But, Mom!"

"Sorry. That's final."

This was a stiletto right through my heart.

Once a year Dhahran threw a fair for the town at the King's Road ball field. Dozens of booths stretched from first base toward the theater. From home base to third was reserved for the donkey rides and the main attraction: the donkey races.

People from the other districts, Dammam and Khobar, came to watch the big parade snake down King's Road. Behind high-stepping majorettes and a loud marching band, trailed legions of scouts from Brownies and Cubs to Eagles, cowgirls and cowboys on fine Arabian horses, floats of all kinds — one with square dancers, another with languid mermaids — dozens of classic cars. Pickups towing speed boats, and a couple of fire trucks with all the lights flashing.

The parade ended at the fairgrounds, already teeming with action. Dozens of booths and makeshift pavilions hosted displays, games, and performances. The Art Club had an exhibit of paintings, and a cartoonist drew funny caricatures in mere minutes. The garden club featured a subtle range of African violets and orchids, the crisply uniformed Girl Scout mothers explained the various merit badges in more detail than most people wanted to hear. The Motorcycle Club guys had a bike with its rear wheel mounted on rollers and throttled it to great delight.

There was a booth where a short, burly driller with a badly chewed, unlit cigar in his mouth would estimate your weight to plus or minus a pound. It cost 4 quirsh. If he missed, he'd give you 20 quirsh or a riyal. He pinned me at 52 pounds and when I stepped on the scale he was dead on. I hung around trying to figure how he did it. He was amazing. I don't think he was wrong one in 20 times.

The airlines and car agencies in Khobar gave out key

chains and quoted prices. There was a sewing circle showing how to make a Raggedy Ann doll that entranced my little sisters. The Women's Group table had free cookies. Here and there, one group or another was selling, for charity, Pepsi out of barrels of ice or those small Dixie cups of ice cream that come with a small wooden spoon, stocked in mini-freezers about waist high.

Built with a parachute for a ceiling, Dramaramco's spacious booth was stocked with actors in costume: Cleopatra, Napoleon, Robin Hood, Mata Hari, Charlie Chaplin, Sherlock Holmes, and the like. They laughed a lot while putting on impromptu skits. The geologists had a pyramid of sawed-in-half geodes and, in glass cases, a display of all the minerals found in Arabia. I focused on the sole gold nugget, committing it to memory for when I next found one. The Yacht Club had a speedboat and a bunch of gleaming water skis leaning against it. The Bowling Club folks wearing their bowling shirts gave out brochures and rulebooks — when they weren't talking to each other.

One of the liveliest pavilions was the Turtle Races. A big tub of water and rocks hosted dozens of small turtles from Hofuf. Each one had a number carefully painted on its shell. The race track was an eight-foot-long sheet of plywood with six furring strips nailed lengthwise for lanes painted red and yellow with blue trim. It was operated by a bunch of old guys, at least 40, who were having a great time, bantering back and forth and handing out turtles to the kids to place in the starting gate.

The announcer was a tall, thin fellow with a crew cut and a golden larynx. He kept up a rapid patter to excite the crowd, and when the gate was lifted, he called it like a pro from Churchill Downs: "Number 7 is in the lead, 14 is coming up fast on the left, in the pack 22 and 3 are neck and neck. Oh, oh, number 7 is turning back in the wrong direction..." and so on, until finally one of the reptiles crossed the finish line, and the next race began. It was great fun for all us kids — and the old guys, too.

There was a lot to enjoy amid this milling crowd. To the Saudis there, I guess that they must have figured that this is the American version of a *suq*, but you can't buy much of anything. *Why is that man in a clown costume sitting above a tank of water? Why are people throwing balls at him? Oh, I see! That's funny! Everybody else is laughing, too.*

BANG! A huge cloud spewed confetti into the air. A merry trio of young mechanics out of the shops had built a four-foot-long air cannon powered by a big compressed-air tank. They had a small coffee can of confetti that, before our eyes, they sprinkled with folded, marked pieces of paper worth a riyal or even five riyals. They shook up the can and loaded the cannon, shouted out a countdown and blasted thousands of tiny pieces of paper over the crowd. We immediately raced about looking for magic confetti, and the three guys toasted each other with their special cups of Pepsi.

All of this — and so much more — I wasn't going to see any of it.

I watched my entire family head off to be in the parade, or watch it, and then go to the fair. Oh well, I went back to my Mitsubishi Zero, read some comics, had a sandwich, and by late afternoon, in the dense oleander hedge along the side of the front lawn, I'm a teenage Hungarian Freedom Fighter about to take out a Soviet tank with a Molotov cocktail... when my mom and sisters come through the gate. My mother is in good spirits when she sees me and says, "Sorry you missed it. If you want, you can go up and look around, but be home in an hour."

"Thanks," and I drop the virtual Molotov cocktail and scamper off to the baseball field a block away. When I arrive, the crowd has evaporated, the donkeys are being loaded on trucks for the ride back to Qatif, and the booths are fairly cleared out, though a few folks are still packing up. I walk to the far end at the theater parking lot, along the row of deserted stalls, checking the confetti for winners and then wander back across the field towards home, thinking about all the cool things I missed.

Ahead, a few adults linger in lawn chairs, happily chatting away, enjoying the early evening breeze and the golden dusk. I pass them, when I spot one of those freezers full of Dixie cup ice cream, standing alone 20 feet away. I rush over, wishing against all hope that there will be one Dixie cup left, preferably strawberry.

You usually don't have to be careful of what you wish for, because you aren't going to get it anyway. I open the abandoned freezer, and it is absolutely empty. No Dixie cups, no shelves either. Just a four-foot-high box with a door. So I close it and open it a few times and then examine the freezer latch more closely. It seems that you can close the door almost completely, and then you can easily open it again. Fascinated, I fool with it some more as the sun sets lower over the King's Road baseball field.

The problem with this kind of idle experimentation is that you can easily convince yourself that you know what you are doing. I can fit into the freezer, so the obvious thing is to get in and close the door almost all the way. Wait a bit and spring out. It will be hilarious.

I climb in the white, molded plastic interior of the box and get comfortable. I've got some room, and this is perfectly doable. I pull in the door by its inner lip until it touches my fingers, gripped around the edge of the freezer. I swing the door back and forth. Seems good to me. I retract my fingers and slowly close the door. At first there is an inch of daylight, but it contracts to a bright sliver. I pull the door just a hair until it is black inside. This is perfect. I'll count to 30 and spring out.

I'm in the dark at 13, when the door opens to let in a crack of light, I pull it back a bit and hear, "Click!"

Click! The sound immediately bypasses all my cognitive faculties and races to the lowest, most primal part of the brain, the almond-sized amygdala —the lizard brain in charge of human survival. The lizard brain says, "Holy Moley! You're smoked. Make the most of it."

I start screaming and banging the sides of the freezer in total blackness. Instantly, I'm in a cold sweat, kicking and yelling, on the edge of total panic — when something makes me stop. I take a short breath, blink in the darkness, and think for a moment about what to do. And then start rocking back forth within the ice box — shrieking and punching the door all the time. The freezer starts to sway, more and more, until it slams me on my back as it falls over.

I'm sort of dazed. This isn't much better than when the freezer was upright, but now it's more comfortable. I'm a little slow and sleepy anyway. I think about that boy Pharaoh in his sarcophagus that I saw in National Geographic. Yikes! The lizard brain kicks in, and I scream and yell and curse, again and again. Too panicked to be scared.

Suddenly, the door opens to clean, clear air and a deep amber dusk. An astonished man with glasses leans over me and says, "Are you all right? I saw it fall over. Are you okay?"

Blitzed by fresh air and daylight, I can't believe that I'm alive. I truly love this man, whoever he is. I blurt out, "No!

Yes! Thank you so much! Thank you. Yes! Bye! Thank you!" and then bolt out of the freezer like a rabid badger freed from a snare.

I streak for home and stumble through the back door into the kitchen. My mom is making dinner. She's startled when she sees me and says, "Tim, you look as white as a ghost. Are you sick? What have you been doing?"

"Nothing," I reply.

And then it hits me. I realize all that I might have lost, beginning with my mother. And I can't hold back the tears.

Willard Drumm 1954

SALT TABLET LAKE

H alf Moon Bay! What can I say?

Living in 1950s Aramco, it was paradise. Not as much for the Ras Tanurans who lived at the beach, but for those us in Dhahran living on the rocky jebel or the citizens of Abqaiq, planted deep within a vast sand dune field thirty miles from the coast, Half Moon Bay spelled happiness.

Aramco began in 1934 as a company called CASOC, a commercial venture between Standard Oil of California and the Saudi government, so it was natural that the company's point men were surveyors and geologists from California. When they first saw this estuary south of Dhahran, they named it Half Moon Bay after the famous beach south of San Francisco.

From the beginning its warm, unspoiled waters lured us all: toddlers, mud castle builders, swimmers, fishermen, sailors, water skiers, snorkelers, and beachgoers of every age. The shore was completely undeveloped, and the beaches as far as you could see were absolutely as pristine as they always had been – not a speck of plastic litter anywhere. Just clean sand bleeding off into the waist-high water for a few yards until sharply descending 15 or 20 feet at the drop-off.

In the summer the water temperature can get into the high 80s, but swim out to the drop-off and dive under about six feet, and you'll hit the thermocline, a sharply defined layer of cooler water, where the temperature drops to the 70s. Cool and refreshing. The entire coastline of Half Moon Bay was pretty much the way it had always been for thousands of years, if not more.

A road had been built across the head of the bay, maybe in the 1940s, leaving to the north a lake several hundred yards long that was cut off from the bay. Salt water kept seeping in, but it never left, and the lake kept getting saltier and saltier. The water was much greener than in the bay, so we called it Salt Tablet Lake in honor of the hallowed salt tablet and the ubiquitous hunter green salt tablet dispensers that were everywhere in Aramco. Every weekend hundreds of adults drove past this great salt lake on the way to the Yacht Club. Hardly any of them bothered to check it out, but we did.

The Salt Tablet was probably saltier than the Dead Sea or the Great Salt Lake in Utah. We'd wade out into four feet of water and sit down to float around as if we were seated in chaise lounges. Go out a little deeper and try to dive to the bottom, and you couldn't do it. No matter how hard you swam, by the time you got past your knees you'd come bobbing back up like a cork.

Of course the hyper salty water would really smart if you had any open cuts, but anything that could sting that sharply must be curative. Ben Michaels claimed that one dunking in the Salt Tablet banished his athlete's foot forever. Smith swore that its waters cured his leprosy in two minutes.

We're all sixteen. Ben, Landis, and I are floating around in the Salt Tablet with Marie and Sheila. Splashing each other, trying to dive down, bobbing around, talking about the party tonight at Barclay's. It's August around two in the afternoon. The temperature is about 125 degrees, and the UV Hazard Index is about 20 points over death ray, so we are obviously having a great time.

The lake begins about 20 feet across the road, and in the mud along the shore, water seeps up from the bay in bubbling geyser pots tinted with salts in shades of green and blue and merges into a thick mud.

The scientific definition of quicksand is a phenomenon where water surfaces up from below, through the sand to make it a quagmire of suspended mud designed to suck you down to your death. So naturally we wiggled into the quicksand near the shore and gradually sank ourselves into the yielding mud. It was cooling once you were in past your calves.

Ben and Landis were bulky guys, so they had to vigorously work their way into the ooze. Sheila wasn't enthusiastic at all about this adventure but gamely settled in well beyond her calves. However, Marie, skinny as a pencil - like Twiggy, thought this was the most fun and quickly sank beneath her waist into the cool mud bath.

Literally embedded in the shore of Salt Tablet lake, under a violent sun without hats, T-shirts or sun screen, we are happily chattering away when Ben relates a story that he had just read.

A French orchid collector in the Amazon stumbles upon a bearded English geologist trapped in quicksand within a pond – inexorably dragged down in the water until only the chin of his upraised face is visible. The man mutters something that the Frenchman can't quite hear, but never mind, this fellow needs immediate help. Looking around for some way to rescue the geologist, he finds a long, heavy moss-covered log and with incredible effort pulls it over and tips it up vertically at the edge of the pond.

The English man's eyes grow large, and speaking carefully, so the water won't spill down his throat, says hoarsely, "Don't make waves," just as the Frenchmen topples the log into the water. It turned out poorly.

It probably wasn't the right story to tell at that time. Suddenly Marie, who was now immersed to her belly button, begins to reconsider. She starts struggling to free herself from the muck. Which of course makes her sink deeper. We're all only a couple of feet from each other, but wiggle as we may, we really aren't extracting ourselves too quickly, and she seems to keep sinking. Marie is getting almost hysterical now, "Guys! Get me out! Now! Please!"

In mud past his knees, Landis, who has an eye out for Marie anyway, tries to bull his way free and rescue her only to get more in mired. Ben is laughing at Landis, as he struggles to use his arms to pull himself out leg by leg with limited success. Marie is panicking, when Sheila, who has quietly finessed herself out of the mud, steps over to Marie, hugs her under the arms, and gradually lifts her free before Ben and Landis can clear their calves from the grasping ooze. So much for their macho self esteem.

Me? I am up to mid-thigh the farthest away from everybody, so I get to watch this unfold like a skit on Saturday Night Live.

Once we are all extricated from the mud, we dive back into the Salt Tablet to clean off, and soaking wet, we head back to the Yacht Club. It's about a half-mile away along the smooth, curving beach of Half Moon Bay. As we walk along, the water quickly evaporates, and we look like five salt-encrusted ghosts drifting along the shore, talking about Barclay's party that night.

Jebel Shamaal - *Willard Drumm 1954*

CLOSE CALL AT JEBEL SHAMAAL

Smith is in the hospital. Despite half a summer spent in the sun, he's as pale as a Norwegian in winter. Beneath his sweaty brow and coke-bottle Buddy Holly glasses an oxygen mask obscures the rest of his face. He's got double-pneumonia at least. The doctors are frightened that he might have a virulent variation of Valley Fever.

I tell him that our plan is in action. He pulls his ventilator mask to one side to confide in me that it's only mononucleosis that he got by making out with Sally G., and then he starts coughing uncontrollably. As if there was an ice cube's chance in Qatif that she would even be seen talking to him. He puts the mask back on, calms down, and mutters, "Have a blast." I leave his room and wander off in a futile search for Sally G.

The next morning we assemble at Ben Michael's house where I meet up with Jim Landis as well as two other miscreants, Walt and Billy K., aka K-man, whom I barely know. We have water and packs of supplies like tuna fish, Danish salami, baked beans, Mars bars, and pistachio nuts, as well as pellet guns, a BB gun, a bunch of firecrackers and bottle rockets and, unknown to us, K-Man has one large cough-syrup bottle of medicinal antiseptic.

Mansoor, who drives Dhahran taxi #10, picks us up. He is a wonderful, big-boned Taifi who is always glad to abet our adventures: drop us off at Half Moon Bay, take us to Qatif or Hofuf to go diving in the wells. He thinks that it is a great idea to drive us to Jebel Shamaal.

All five of us hop into the big Chevy Impala. The jebel is a little north of Dhahran on the Ras Tanura road. We drive a bit, and then Mansoor hangs a left and fish-tails the cab two miles down the sand road with Radio Bozuki at full blast. He drops us off near the jebel, promises to pick us up tomorrow about four and rides off thinking, *These American kids are crazy. They want to spend an August day in the desert?* He cranks his AC to high and speeds off.

At 509 feet high Jebel Midra Ash-Shamaal is the second tallest free-standing peak on the eastern coast of the Gulf from Kuwait to Abu Dhabi, Jebel Midra Al-Junubi, a few miles to the south, was skinnier but two feet higher until a dozen years ago when a cartel of wretched opportunists leveled it to the ground to sell its rock. But that is another story.

Massive, basically conical mountains standing alone in the desert, they were both capped with limestone that had once blanketed the land, now eroded hundreds of feet down to the desert, leaving only the twin pinnacles.

We make our way up to Jebel Shamaal's broad base and cross to the slope, checking out the caves and jackal dens along the way. Climbing over great broken slabs of limestone, tasting bitter, red berries from an unknown plant, snapping off and crushing between our fingernails tiny, pungent wild peppers, scanning the ground for arrow heads and flint hand-axes like some of the Exploration guys had found in the Rub' al-Khali.

We had heard that there was a cave with a ceiling covered in stone-age stick figures. Lizards skitter off into the rocks; we round the edge of a broken cliff and surprise a giant vulture resting in the shade. With a great flapping noise it unfolds its eight-foot wing span and flies off. K-man lifts his pellet gun for a shot, but Ben waves him down, and we watch the great bird soar into a thermal and ascend in a wide corkscrew pattern until it is only a black speck in the sky.

Finally at the top, we put down our packs and pass around the canteens. We can see everything in every direction. Jebel Dhahran to the east, far below tiny cars and trucks ply the two-lane blacktop, to the west there is nothing but endless desert stretching thirty miles into the horizon. South stands Jebel Junnubi, and farther on there are rocky ridges drifted with sand and scrubby bushes that meld into the desert floor.

Ben is a tall, rangy guy with an infinite enthusiasm for skin diving and outdoor misadventures of all sorts. Dressed like all of us in cut-off Levis and a white T-shirt, he whips out the diving knife strapped to his calf and carves off hunks of salami which makes us even thirstier. Better have some pistachio nuts, too. The Mars bars are soft and all but melted into pudding, but we tear open an end of the wrapper and squish out the chocolate like a tube of frosting. Now we are ready for the shooting expedition. We have four single-shot, spring-powered pellet guns well made by the Diana company in Germany, and I have a holstered gas-powered, repeating BB pistol as well as a variety of fireworks.

Making our way down the jebel we spread out into the surrounding desert. Ben, Landis, the missing Smith, and I are lifelong friends who have spent days together skin diving, camping out or roaming in the desert. Landis is an athletic kid with a great wit and, for some reason not apparent to any of us, considered quite good-looking by the girls. Walt and Billy K. didn't get out of camp much. Walt is thin, sturdy and even-tempered, but K-Man is a bit twitchy.

Invited as a favor to Landis, who has the hots for Billy's sister, the lanky kid's eyes dart around so much that you wonder if he is looking for some demon about to pull the tilt switch. At 17, he is a year older than us but acts like an adolescent. He also has a slight goiter and has a way of contorting his back every once in a while as if his spine is having a hiccup.

Walt and Billy K. blast away at every lizard, dung beetle, and grasshopper they encounter without hitting any of them. In search of bigger prey, the three of us walk on. Landis is the first to catch the scent; he signals to us to spread out, and quietly we creep up on our victim.

Not fifteen feet away in a patch of sand fringed with salt grass, unaware of its impending fate, an intact, weathered Tuborg ginger-ale bottle is pinned neck down in a gnarled bush. Landis fires first. His pellet pings the glass and ricochets, I follow with the same result, and then Ben, who has a Diana 35, the most powerful pellet gun, hits the bottle straight on. End of the hunt. We inspect the carnage and search for more species that we can endanger.

Not five minutes later Ben spots a rusted, gallon-size ghee can thirty feet away hiding in a pile of broken rocks. He fires immediately before it can bolt, and we follow suit. After a fusillade of pellets and BBs, Ben finally hits the can in the seam and splits it open. Before we can inspect the trophy, K-Man starts hollering. We turn to see him a dozen yards behind us jumping up and down, shouting, "Snake! Snake!"

We run over to find Walt poking at the creature with a long stick. It is a snake all right – about a foot long, skinny as a fat pencil. It coils and wiggles, spitting out its tongue and snapping its jaws in defiance.

"Jeez, it's a pit viper," I say.

"Let's kill it," says Billy K. and shoots his rifle. Walt fires, too. And the unharmed viper slithers quickly into the rocks.

K-Man drops his rifle, goes down on his knees and lunges after the snake, "I can get it."

Landis comes out of nowhere and knocks him to the ground. "It's a pit viper, damn it!" Thinking, *His sister will kill me if I return him with a paralyzed central nervous system.*

"What's a pit viper?" he says.

Landis rolls his eyes, and we crack up. K-Man says, "Is it like a cobra?" This is even funnier.

We disperse to walk quietly around in the desert, comfortable with its stony ridges drifted with sand, sprouting tufts of stunted grass. Shallow ravines eroded into the earth to reveal different layers of time – bands of tiny pebbles interspersed with layers of dark mud or pale chert peppered with tiny shells. Then there are those big dried-out bushes, practically dead, that make you wonder how they ever managed to grow to the size of a refrigerator. If you linger and stare at one of those bushes for a few minutes you will begin to notice the teeming world of bugs, flies, hopping creatures, beetles, and ants that live together beneath its shade.

Eventually the sun begins to set, and we drift back to the jebel. Billy K. is still a little antsy. By now he is shooting at large boulders that are impossible to miss. Ben and I take the lead and are about forty yards up the slope when K-Man shoots Ben in the back.

It's not really a big deal. The range was long, and it didn't more than sting him, but it ignites a pellet-gun war.

To those who ran in different circles when they were young and aren't conversant with the etiquette of a pellet-gun war, the object isn't to hit the opponent in a vital area but to get fairly close, and if there is a shot at an exposed shin, take it.

So Ben shoots back at K-Man, and Walt returns the favor. I fire off the repeating BB pistol, a hopelessly inaccurate weapon, but its hail of BBs make Landis and Walt duck. Ben fires again and hits Billy K. in the thigh. He starts jumping around and twitching his spine at the same time. We all break out laughing. Ben shouts, "Let's twist again, like we did last summer," and then Landis wings a pellet my way.

It's getting darker. I'm halfway up the hill but wedge myself into a cleft of the mountain and lay out my fireworks on the chest-high rock ledge in front of me. I balance my bottle rockets pointing down and light off all five of them.

It's glorious. In the dying light they streak down and explode all around our enemy. Ben keeps shooting, but he's three against one, so I fire another round of BBs and then start lighting the fireworks in front of me and throwing them down the hill like grenades.

You should know that there are three kinds of firecrackers. Ladyfingers, which are tiny one-inch-long noisemakers, are virtually useless unless you light off a whole string in the movie theater.

Then there is the standard firecracker about as big as your little finger, packed in strings of twenty for three riyals. Each firecracker contains a significant amount of gunpowder, and any semi-industrious kid can break open a whole string and collect a pile of the explosive – the first step to creating an ingenious exploding device.

At the top of the heap is the Blockbuster. The size of a Cuban cigar, this is a serious piece of ordnance easily capable of launching a galvanized-steel garbage can lid several feet into the air. At ten riyals apiece, they are saved for special occasions. I've got three of them as well as two strings of firecrackers on the ledge right in front of me.

I light a Blockbuster but accidentally light the fuse near the middle and the front half of sizzling fuse falls off. It's now a short-fused bomb, and I quickly throw it into an arc where it explodes just over Walt's head and briefly silhouettes him in a bright flash. I laugh.

I look down. The other part of the burning fuse has fallen on the string of firecrackers and BOOM, BOOM, BOOM. They are exploding, pinning me against the rock; wedged in, I can't run, and they are blowing up in my face. A Blockbuster goes off amid the exploding firecrackers, and the sonic boom nearly bounces my head off the rock. I see the remaining Blockbuster with a sputtering fuse roll off the ledge into the cracked fissure I'm standing in. I plant my hands and leap vertically just as the giant firecracker goes off. It's my turn to be lit up like an epileptic puppet in the sudden flash.

Down below, they think this is hysterically funny. Ben does too, but he lets off a round at them anyway. They return fire, and the skirmish resumes for about half a minute, and then from below there is some whispering. They aren't shooting back.

Walt shouts, "Landis is hit."

"Oh sure. Nice try." Ben yells back.

"No, really. He's bleeding all over."

"Why didn't you say so? I'm coming down." Ben picks his way down the jebel in the deepening dusk. I follow and, sure enough, Landis is bleeding all over his T-shirt pressed over his right eye.

A frightened Walt is standing close to him, not sure what to do. Billy K. is doing that twitch thing with his back a few paces away.

"Landis! Are you okay?

He raises his head and with a lopsided grin says, "I surrender. You're a terrible shot. You missed my eye by two inches." He laughs faintly and then goes slack and begins to pass out before Ben catches him. After a minute we get Jim to his feet and start back up to the top of the jebel. The sun is down, and the early moon is on the horizon, but it's still very dark. We carefully pick our way over the rocks, up sand drifts, and around thoroughly dead woody shrubs bristling with sharp twigs as nasty as cactus.

Walt is a good scout for Ben and me as we guide Landis up to the summit. We stop for a moment, and Jim seems coherent. Billy K. is a bit behind us, and no one is thinking about him when we hear a stifled scream. "Arrrrgh…" and then a whispered "Ahh… Help… Ahh…"

We put Landis down and scramble over in the direction of the voice. There is a whimpering in the shadows. Ben lights a match, and splayed before us is K-Man.

He has stumbled on a root. Figured that he'd just jump over it - and launched himself onto a nasty, twiggy bush about the size of a patio table. He is suspended off the ground like one of those Indian holy men on a bed of nails. He can't talk very distinctly because his throat as well as the rest of his body is punctured by dozens of tiny cactus-like thorns.

"Ahhh, ahhh…" he moans, and the match goes out. He rasps, "Ahhh, ahhh…" in the dark.

Ben lights another match. We fully comprehend Billy's situation, sprawled face-down over this woody clump barely able to speak. We look at each other and dissolve into hysterics. It is the funniest thing we have ever seen. Of course we have compassion for our fellow man, K-Man included, but when he groans, "Ahhh, ahhh…" again, we crack up even more.

Finally we regain our composure and apply ourselves. Ben will take an arm, I'll grab a leg, from the other side Walt will take Billy's shoulder, and we'll lift him up and off the bush. A perfect plan but Walt loses his grip, and we sort of drag K-Man over the spiny shrub. He is rolling around in the sand, cursing and pulling out thorns but it isn't as bad as if he had fallen into a real cactus. We go back to get Landis. When we tell him what happened, he starts laughing like a guy who didn't have a pellet in his eyebrow.

As the crescent moon rises in the black sky, brilliantly diffused with all the stars and galaxies of the Milky Way, we reach our camp at the top. It's a fantastic panoramic view, but Landis needs some attention. We settle him down on a sleeping bag spread on a big, flat slab of rock. K-Man has recovered from his multiple punctures, so I ask him to gather some dry brush to make a fire behind a wind-sheltered rock. He goes to it with a bitter vengeance against dry vegetation.

With a crackling blaze lighting us up, we stand around Landis. Ben uses his diving knife to cut some more salami, and we pass around the water. Then he takes his knife and slices into a can of beans, which he props next to the fire. We are watching the concoction heat, wondering whether we should have removed the paper label which is now cindering its way into the beans. Landis moans.

By now I have a flashlight, and Landis is sitting up on the rock. "We've got to do something," he says. "Look at it."

So we lay him back on the sleeping bag and peel the T-shirt from his eye. The pellet has flattened itself on the bone of his upper-right eyebrow almost exactly two inches above his eyeball, which is considerably less durable. We can see the lump, but Ben pokes it with his finger, and Landis lets out a yell. "God, Landis, I'm sorry. It was definitely the Diana 35."

"A primo pellet gun, but we gotta do something," he whispers.

We think about what to do for a minute before Ben pulls out his diving knife and says, "I'll have to cut it out, or you'll die of lead poisoning."

None of us, Landis included, has considered the lead poisoning angle until just now, and Jim, obviously conflicted, is semi-convinced by this learned medical opinion. I'm thinking that surgical intervention might be a little sketchy, but we have to do something. I say to Billy K., "Where's that cough medicine you said you had." He rummages in his pack and brings out the standard size, squared-off Aramco cough medicine bottle filled with a clear antiseptic and hands it to me.

You can't be too sure about the purity of these potions, so I take a swig, hand the bottle to Walt who has a swallow and passes it to Ben. K-Man wants a hit, but Walter tells him it will inflame his puncture wounds.

Landis takes a pull, and then screams a little as I pour some tonic over his wound. I give him another taste. Ben wipes his knife against the leg of his jeans and says, "I'll have to sterilize the scalpel," takes the bottle and pours the contents over the blade.

We're gathered around Landis lying on the limestone slab. The fire is flickering shadows around the crest of the mountain, the moon is rising higher, and the horizon is nothing but darkness sprinkled with stars. There is hardly any breeze when Ben lights a match and ignites his diving knife.

Jim is semi-dazed on his back, but his eyes get really big when Ben thrusts the flaming blade above his head and shouts out an oath to Odin, of all people. Then Ben waves his hand to put out the flame, but it persists, and flailing the knife wildly, he burns his thumb before it's extinguished. He puts a moistened fingertip to the steel, and it sizzles. The surgeon is ready to operate. Ben approaches the terrified Landis.

I'm flashing on that picture from Bible class of Abraham sacrificing Isaac and in a rare moment of good judgment say, "We better not operate. It might get infected."

Ben seems to be a little disappointed, but he is actually relieved because he has no idea of how to dissect Landis' eyebrow to get the pellet out. He was planning to wing it after the first incision. "Okay, let's get him to the hospital."

As we gather our packs the wind kicks up, and Billy K. throws a bush the size of a kettledrum onto the fire. It bursts into a giant fireball, showering us with sparks and tiny embers as we start down the hill. The moon and our flashlights illuminate the way. Landis is leaning on Ben, Walt and I are leading the way, and no one cares where K-Man might be.

We make it down the hill okay and walk a bit on the dirt road before we see a Bedouin tent lit up with Coleman lanterns, a stake-body truck parked in front. A kid spots us coming and scampers off to get his parents. Two men come out from the tent, and they are highly skeptical.

We are all carrying rifles, I have a holstered pistol on my hip, and we are supporting Landis, the blood-red T-shirt pressed over his eye. It takes these guys about two seconds to realize that Landis needs help, and two minutes later we are all on our way to Dhahran in the truck. At the Main Gate, the driver knows the guard so we go directly to the hospital and appear at the Emergency Room about one in the morning.

Walt and K-Man immediately evaporate, and Ben stays with our stuff while I go in with Landis. Everyone is very helpful, they whisk him away, and now all I have to do is call Max Landis and tell him why his son is in the ER.

This is sort of a problem because I can't very well say that Ben drilled him with an exquisite shot from a decent range. I can't blurt out that at least he didn't get hit in the eyeball. While the phone rings and rings I consider the best way to break the news and then a sleepy Max answers, "Who's this?

"Mr. Landis. This is Tim."

"Do you know what time…What is it?"

"Ah… Ah… Jim got shot in the head."

"What?"

I probably could have phrased it better, but Mr. Landis was a fierce personality, and I got rattled. He is now completely undone and racing to the hospital. Ben and I decide that we are no longer needed and flee before Max arrives.

It turns out that the area above the eyebrow is riddled with countless muscles, tiny nerves, blood vessels and the like. Who knew? Extracting a lead pellet from the cranial brow is a delicate procedure. Had Ben operated, Landis would have had a dead right eyebrow for life, but somehow he would have pulled off that look.

The next morning, Smith is alone in his hospital bed, still breathing heavily through the ventilator mask when his dad comes in with a serious face and says, "I've got bad news. Something terrible happened to Jim Landis."

Magnified by his thick lenses, Smith's beady eyes grow narrow with interest, and he says, though the mask muffles his voice a bit, "What happened?"

"They were at Jebel Shamaal. Going back up to the top, Jim tripped and nearly shot himself in the eye."

Smith immediately knows exactly what happened. He starts to hoarsely giggle but stifles it - for about ten seconds - before he bursts out laughing so hard in the oxygen mask that he almost asphyxiates, before he can pull it from his face.

* * *

A few days later Smith recovers and is returned to society. A plan quickly evolves. It's Thursday, and tonight there is a Tri-D in Ras Tanura. During the summer each district hosted a big dance for all the returning students in Aramco. It's easy to imagine just how much fun four hundred, barely supervised teenagers dancing to rock and roll can have.

I'm headed to Smith's house; we're going to see *Dracula's Sister* at the one o'clock Thursday matinee and then catch the bus to RT. Smith's mom Lilian answers the door. She's warm enough, but I can detect a lingering animosity regarding a certain giant gingerbread boy whose head was mysteriously bitten off as it cooled on the kitchen table. I was falsely accused of this crime.

Smith comes out and we adjourn to his room, he locks the door and says, "Check this out," as he pulls his Aramco bag out of the closet. It's packed with a towel, a change of clothes, his swim suit, and actually more stuff than anyone would need for a night in RT. He roots around in the bag and brings out a small mayonnaise jar containing a clear fluid.

"Wicked. Did you get it from Rocky?" Rocky Desmond was a stout, awkward kid whose dad operated a mini-refinery at home with poor inventory control.

"No. Rocky couldn't deliver, so I got it from my dad's stash. He'll never know because I poured in some water."

"Brilliant. We'll have a great time," and then Smith puts the jar back into his Aramco bag.

I say, "No, don't put it in the bag. Hide it. And then we can get it when we leave."

"Oh, no. It's fine. Let's go to the movie."

So we go to the movie. It's fairly cheesy, but Dracula's sister is a knockout, and there's some good action. After the show we return to Smith's to get his bag and then catch the bus to RT. He opens the back door, and we step into the kitchen to meet one seriously angry mother. She doesn't have to say a word: we know that we are thoroughly doomed.

"How could you do this to me, to your dad?"

In a brave attempt at valor under fire, Smith says, "Did what? I didn't do anything."

Her withering look could melt sand into glass. "I went to put a fresh T-shirt in your bag and found the jar."

Of course this is not news to us. It only confirms our worst nightmare. She's furious. "You, you. Your father could lose his job. How could you?" and then she starts crying. "He is in the living room." And we trudge into the Nuremberg trials.

Smoking his pipe, a very somber Mr. Smith glowers at us and says, "You two are in deep trouble. Transporting between the districts is a serious crime. It could result in our overnight expulsion from the kingdom." Something that had never occurred to us. Didn't Mr. Smith take a special thermos along when he went fishing with John Ames?

"Tim, go out on the back porch while I talk to Smith alone." Even his dad called him Smith.

So I wait on the porch until Smith signals that it's my turn in the barrel. The Smiths are great friends with my parents. Ray Smith is really a good guy and a connoisseur of detective novels. He and my mom often chatter away about Perry Mason and Agatha Christie novels that they had read. Now he is very stern-looking, but completely into his detective mode. He tells me again the potential disastrous consequences of our stupidity, how my parents will be embarrassed of me and finally gets to the one question that he really wants to ask, "Where did you get the stuff?"

Without blinking, I reply, "Rocky Desmond."

He stares at me, takes a puff of his pipe and says, "Go get Smith."

We are standing as repentant as it is possible to be without getting on our knees, as Ray reads us the riot act and finally closes by saying, "Thanks to each of you, for being honest about who gave you the stuff. You two are really lucky that you didn't drink Rocky's stuff. I sampled it— it's probably the worst rot gut ever made. You'd be better off drinking camel piss."

He is describing his own blend, what he calls "the best taste in camp." Smith and I are gritting our teeth trying to contain ourselves. Then Ray says, "It's barely second run. It could have blinded you or even paralyzed you. It's pure poison."

At that we practically bite off the tips of our tongues trying to prevent an outburst of maniacal laughter. We don't dare look at each other, or it'll be over. Somehow we maintain a contrite appearance, and finally Mr. Smith delivers the verdict. Smith is not going to the Tri-D ever and is grounded for a very long time.

He turns to me and says, "I'm not one of those parents who call up your dad and tattle on you. You're a young man now. I know that you will tell your dad what happened and let him decide. I'll leave it up to you." Up to me? My dad will never hear a whisper. I gracefully exit through the kitchen, past Lillian's gaze of death — as if I had corrupted her precious innocent child, and out into the alley.

I've missed the bus to RT, so I'm hanging around the house when the phone rings. "Barger, my parents just went out to a party. Call a cab and pick me up."

"We don't have enough money to take a cab to RT."

"We'll have him take us to the main gate and hitch a ride."

A perfect plan. I immediately agree, blithely dismissive of the fact that Smith's parents will boil him alive. Not much later, around dusk, we are standing on the road opposite of the main gate with our thumbs out. It's a little slow before a battered flat-bed truck passes by and stops about twenty yards away. We sprint for the truck, but Smith's lungs are still recovering; by time we make it to the truck, he is wheezing like he's having some kind of asthma attack. The driver waves us on board, and we climb onto a pile of cement bags in the open bed. It is a bit breezy as we lay back on the dusty, 100-pound paper sacks, but we have a perfect view of the sun setting over the desert between Dhahran and Ras Tanura. It's dark when we arrive at the RT main gate and get a ride from some kind American to the Surf House, the camp's main recreational complex on the beach of the Gulf. The Tri-D has been going on for a while, and we can hear the music throbbing as we pass a few kids lingering outside.

Surf music was the craze and a natural theme for the RT Tri-D. The main hall was cleared into a giant dance floor, decorated with murals of surfers and giant waves. A generous use of palm fronds added to the décor, and the sound system was seriously loud. One of the organizers had called Housing to order the delivery of a couple hundred seat cushions made for those big sturdy Aramco-issue maple sofas. Now, they were piled along the edge of the dance floor.

We step into the vast room. There are three adult couples at a table near the door cringing at the music, trying to remember why they volunteered to chaperone. Beyond them is Teenage Babylon. Hundreds of couples dancing to the Beach Boys, the Surfaris, or Dick Dale and the Deltones on a dark dance floor lit by strobing buoy lights borrowed from the Marine department. Along the wall the cushions have melted into sofas for lounging kids – chattering, laughing, smoking Salems, and drinking Pepsi.

All the dancers are moving and shifting together like some giant amoeba. Occasionally someone bursts through the crowd with a particularly intricate move to universal approval. The humid air is thick with smoke and expectations. At some point, Smith is stretched out on some cushions trying to get cozy with this girl from Abqaiq, when a flashlight shines into his face. It's one of the chaperones. "Mr. Smith in Dhahran called. He's looking for his son. Is that you?"

"Smith? Oh…Oh, I just saw him over there," and he points across the room into the writhing mass of dancing teenagers.

"Thanks. I'll take a look," says the man as he wanders off with his flashlight to return to the safety of the chaperone's table. And the wild party goes on and on.

* * * *

A dozen years later it's 1977. At 28 I'm an actual adult and back in Ras Tanura. I've started a video electronics company in Jeddah and, ironically enough, I'm the only legitimate agent for video programming in a Saudi Arabia awash in pirated movies. I've been invited by Aramco to visit the districts and submit a bid for video entertainment.

I take a glorious helicopter ride to an offshore rig in Sufaniyah to check out their video set up. When I return, the sky is darkening. By time I finish the office meetings and go for my rental, a new silver Chevy Impala station wagon, I'm in the middle of a fierce monsoonal rain storm. As I leave the main gate, the rain is coming down so hard the windshield wipers can't keep up with the deluge. I'm about a mile out, speeding down the road, when I hit an enormous pot hole that is so filled with water that I couldn't see it. There is a bone-jarring THUNK, and I drive on.

About halfway to Dhahran the rain stops, and I drive along through the freshly drenched desert. The sun comes out, and the landscape looks vivid and clean. Closer to Dhahran I can see Jebel Shamaal in the distance. By now the Saudi Air Force has militarized the mountain and capped its peak with a geodesic radar dome, but I can only see its general shape on the horizon and a faint rainbow pointing its way.

Cruising along at a good clip, listening to English pop music on Radio Kuwait, I get stuck behind a giant

Mercedes truck piled high with wooden crates. Every time I pull out to pass, some car or pickup truck appears in the other lane, and I have to slow up and fall back behind the truck. I have no reason to hurry, but I'm getting impatient and keep trying to pass.

Finally there is an opening. Sure, another Mercedes freightliner is coming towards me, but there is room to make my move. I pull out to pass the truck but the driver speeds up, making it difficult to get clearance. The other truck is bearing down on me, and it's too late to fall back, so I mash the accelerator and am going about 90 miles an hour as I zoom past the truck and veer back into my lane just in time to avoid the freighter barreling at me.

I make it with about fifty yards to spare and am congratulating myself on a brilliant bit of driving, executed perfectly, when there is a huge CLUNK and a loud screeching sound as my right front wheel breaks off, and I go careening off the road at high speed. Fortunately it's Arabia, so the shoulder blends right into the desert. I'm bouncing around. My hands are fused to the steering wheel as the station wagon plows through bushy hillocks and deep sand to come to a stop 200 feet off the road. The trucker blows his horn as he passes.

I'm stunned. If the wheel had failed 20 seconds earlier, I'd be road kill. Or, even worse, if the left front wheel had snapped instead, I would have been the lunch meat in a

Mercedes Benz truck sandwich. This is all very disturbing. I hyperventilate for a few minutes before I can pry my fingers off the steering wheel and get out of the car to inspect the damage. The wheel is still on the axle, but the suspension is gone, and the right front end rests directly on the shredded, blown-out tire. That pothole must have cracked the shock absorber, and it completely sheered thirty miles later – 100 yards after my artful maneuver.

I look beyond the crippled station wagon to the road. A bright yellow Datsun cab zips by, and all is quiet. Not a car in sight. I turn around to see that I'm directly opposite the looming peak. I think of Ben, invoking a Nordic deity, waving his flaming diving knife over a terrified Landis. Yes, it's another close call at Jebel Shamaal.

Qatif oasis – *Les Snyder 1939*

BENEATH THE OASIS

There is stupid, and then there is another category even dumber than stupid. When I was seventeen, I was pretty much the poster child for beyond stupid. It wasn't entirely my fault. I was more than six feet tall, weighed maybe 170 pounds, and had the body fat of a praying mantis - except for that gram of fat on the pathway between my frontal lobe and my cerebral cortex.

The frontal lobe is where all of your senses are integrated to assess any situation and pass the info back to the rest of the brain where your judgment resides. The traffic light is red, the main brain is signaled, it identifies a stoplight and tells you to stop.

Unfortunately for me, this misplaced gob of fat in the neural path sometimes garbles the message – "Maybe I can pink the light," and other times blocks the message completely, and I jumped off the shed roof with a beach umbrella because I was sure it would make a perfect parachute. Today was one of those days.

Ben and I are in a palm grove in Qatif, watching an artesian well bubbling up clear water into a shallow pool that flows off into a web of canals. The well shaft is about four feet wide. We have decided that it is an excellent idea to dive into this hole with scuba tanks to see how deep it is and where it goes. So we have masks, fins, air tanks and regulators, diving knives, depth gauges, underwater flashlights, and a stunning disregard for the fact that this is one of those plans entirely devoid of an upside. Maybe the only upside is that you survive.

We're prepping our gear, scoping out the well and discussing what special technique we'll apply to this dive. We decide that we'll flip a ten quirsh piece to see who goes first. Suited up, fins in hand, we splash over to the well and, before the coin toss, a problem arises.

Ben is a wide-shouldered, big-chested guy; add the geometry of his scuba tank, and he is basically the same size as the well's diameter. But I'm skinny rather than wide, and I use an unusual scuba tank. Made out of spun aluminum, about a third smaller in diameter and a little longer than the standard size, this lightweight tank once held some kind of exotic industrial gas and was salvaged out of Aramco's reclamation yard. Though it held less air, my techniques of breath control were superb, and I could outlast anyone with a regular tank.

We don't need to flip the coin, and I pull on my mask, sit in the pool to slip on my fins, put in my regulator's mouthpiece, and plunge headfirst into the shaft. I have about ten inches of space all around me as I head downward.

The water is flowing over me like a gentle breeze. It's lukewarm and clear as gin when I turn on my flashlight. The wall of the well is engraved with the chisel marks and gouges made by some tireless men working about the time of Hammurabi. Foot after foot as I submerge, the scratches and counter-chiseled hatch marks begin to speak to me, much as I imagine the brush strokes of an original Van Gogh might do to a perceptive viewer. Of course, at this time I have no such sensitivity and think Don Martin of MAD magazine is a way better artist than Picasso.

I'm headfirst, about ten feet down when it occurs to me that I might have some difficulty getting out of this tube backwards. I stop and see if I can swim in reverse. It's not real efficient, but using my hands I can push myself backwards. When I surface Ben can pull me out of the hole by my ankles. Okay. Problem solved. Let's see what is down here.

Following the beam of the flashlight, I go deeper. It's really quite soothing. The water wafting by, the total quiet only punctuated by a burst of air bubbles.

I check my depth gauge to see that I'm down to thirty feet. Looking at the rock intaglio on the wall, I think about the original excavators digging away with crude tools in a cramped space, filling a hide bucket that is winched to the surface, never knowing when, or if, they would strike the aquifer.

Then I start to reconsider this backward swimming thing. *Maybe this isn't the greatest idea. Oh well, go a little deeper.* A few feet later I'm startled by the low tone of a gong when my tank bangs into the wall. Sound travels well in water, and I float there as the tank resonates. It is close in here after all.

Did I damage the valve? What if I did? Better check. I snake my right arm over my shoulder to check the fitting between the air hose and the tank with my fingers. It seems good. There is no air leaking out. It's okay.

I descend another ten feet to discover a wonderful thing.

The shaft has expanded into a bell-like grotto about five feet wide. I swim into it and turn myself around facing the surface. Now whatever happens, I'm good to go. I pan the flashlight around the chamber's wall carved with the handiwork of men that maybe lived two thousand years ago. The floor is bare rock with a few stones lying around. Breathing softly, I'm relaxed and feeling pretty good, so I turn off the flashlight.

Caressed by the warm artesian water in total darkness, I ease into the fetal position suspended in the chamber like a pea in a pod. I'm free-floating forty feet beneath the surface of the earth in an ancient well shaft.

I put out my arm and feel the wall, reading the etched surface as if it were a language that I didn't speak, written in braille. It's very relaxing like a total immersion hot tub. I drift off a bit before I get this strange feeling as if I am a kind of embryo gestating beneath the earth. At this age I'm totally insensitive to any kind of Zen-like sensibility, but it was that kind of moment.

Oh, oh, I better check my watch. I turn on the flashlight to see that it's 15 minutes later, time to go. I swim upwards. About five yards from the surface, I standby for ten minutes just to be safe.

When you standby to decompress in the offshore oil field at Sufaniya, after breathing through a long air hose for two hours, you are usually hanging onto a length of barnacled pipe attached to an offshore well. As you float there staring at a piling, your throat dry as a fly's eye, you start to zero in on a world of tiny neon fish and tinier marine organisms that dart around the maws of the barnacles—right before your face mask. Bivalves the size of pearls with their shells partially open straining the water for biota. Weird little anemones dangle their languid limbs in the current. Poke towards them with your finger, and they retract into a ball before you can touch them.

So now I'm standing by in the well, 15 feet under, checking out the wall around me. It's perfectly round. In a way this entire shaft is a sculpture worthy of Henry Moore. I can see where a hard edge was rounded taking a pit of rock behind it. Here the vertical gouge of a pickax scores a mark two feet down the wall. I pull out my diving knife and scratch at the rock. It's pretty hard stuff. It must have taken forever to dig this thing. Time is up, and I surface.

A worried, agitated Ben is pacing around surrounded by half a dozen Qatifi farm workers when I pop out of the hole, pull myself into the shallow pool, remove my mouthpiece and lift my mask.

"Where have you been?" Wildly pointing at his diving watch, "You were down there more than forty minutes." Suddenly Ben stops being frantic, breaks into a grin and says, "Jeez, am I glad to see you."

I blink my eyes a couple of times. I hear the palm fronds rustling in the wind and the chitter of field sparrows. I'm dazzled by the thick blue sky, the verdant colors of the date oasis. Green fronds and brown tree trunks in every hue. Golden ripe dates clustered overhead. A fat bee slowly buzzes right past my eyes. The fresh air and faint scents of the garden fill my lungs. The lean, wrinkled farm workers are all smiles – relieved that I hadn't drowned. A cold claw runs down my spine as I suddenly realize that I am so relieved, too.

"Barger? Are you okay?"

"Oh. I'm fine," I say, looking back at the dark mouth of the well, "I'll never do that again." And I didn't.

Dhahran 1967 - *Courtesy of Duane Robinson*

EXCELSIOR!

Dhahran camp ends at 3rd Street – they'd start building the new school there next year. However, the perimeter fence extends way east toward Al-Khobar to enclose more than a square mile of desert that was exactly the same as it ever was. Flat gravelly ground with rocky outcrops drifted with sand, clumps of bushes abound – some dead, some dying. Hillocks formed in the lee of a few big, hearty shrubs sprout tufts of tall, thin grass with a randomness that resembles a hair implant procedure gone terribly wrong.

Nine-year-olds, four-and-a-half feet tall, about 70 pounds each, Milt, Danny and I are prowling around our domain: chasing lizards, throwing rocks at each other, tracking big, black stink beetles, swatting at flies and hovering bees, looking for snakes. Danny has just arrived from New Jersey. Though he is a newcomer, he's a good guy with similar interests: slingshots, blow guns, firecrackers, and an aversion to adult supervision.

Short, cocky with a winning smile, his hair is sculpted with Brylcreem into a semi-pompadour that puts our primitive bowl cuts to shame. It is a cool winter afternoon, so Milt and I are wearing thick, cotton coats, but Danny is wearing his "pride and joy": a black leather motorcycle jacket that was way too small for his brother but is just exactly two sizes too big for Danny.

He wore it always, even on the hot days. It had buckles and zippers everywhere. Out in the desert he told us how he'd fallen backwards off the top of the big slide up at recreation and was saved from breaking any bones by the miraculous leather jacket.

Naturally, acres of empty desert at the edge of the enormous construction project called Dhahran would attract scores of truckloads of rubble, debris and project leftovers – so there are hundreds of broken cinder blocks, strips of galvanized tin, lumber, pipes, and wire of all types scattered everywhere. Scavenging this debris was one of the main attractions of this place.

Milt finds a yard-long piece of electrical conduit piping shaped like a flat S. He shakes off the dirt and blows on it like a trumpet. A plug of dirt blasts out the other end, followed by a flat squeal. He works with it a bit before he's able to play sort of a tune which none of us can recognize. He's delighted and announces that it is a Seussaphone, a Dr. Seuss-a-phone. Danny says that it sounds like an octopus farting.

Interspersed over the landscape are piles of empty wooden crates each about the size of a clothes drier, stenciled on the side with shipping details and the flowing logo of *The Santini Brothers*. Looking back, it should have read *The Extremely Fortunate, "Get down on your knees and praise the Madonna," Santini Brothers*. Based, like Danny, in New Jersey, one of the brothers got a phone call from Aramco's New York office in the late '40s. A logistics manager introduced himself and asked, "Could you consolidate personal effects shipments for our employees in America, crate them up and ship them to Dammam, Saudi Arabia?"

Whatever Santini Brother it was who answered the phone, maybe it was Gino, immediately replied, "Of course we can. We are ready to start tomorrow." And the Santini Brothers handled tens of thousands of personal effects shipments to Saudi Arabia for at least 25 years.

In the old days of the thirties and forties it could easily take half a month to travel back from Arabia to the US, so every employee was given a three-month transcontinental vacation for him and his family, every two years.

At the time, well into the 50s, the Aramco towns were islands in a barren desert, and, beyond the basics, there wasn't much available locally. Khobar was a growing retail center but still not up to speed for American tastes, so Aramco also paid for one generous personal effects shipment every other year.

Thus began the sublime ritual of "The Shipment."

Anyone who lived through those years will understand the significance of this process. The Sears catalog would arrive. It featured everything in America that was for sale, stuff that we never imagined even existed, and it was devoured by everyone in the house. My dad Tom would check out the power tools and fishing rods, my sisters would look at the dollhouses and daydream about wide-lapelled, polka-dot, party dresses with matching hats. I was lost in the 16-page toy section trying to determine if the potato gun was a better deal than the bow-and-arrow set. It was obvious that any kid could pull the suction cups off the arrows and replace them with crude arrowheads fashioned out of the lid of a sardine can.

But none of this really mattered because it was my mom Kathleen who placed the order, and she bought useful products to operate a household with six kids. Once she mailed the check to Sears, it would be forever before the goods would arrive, so all of us — even my parents — gradually forgot about the objects of our desires.

About five months later, out of thin air, like magic, six or seven crates from the Santini Brothers appear in our front yard. The shipment has arrived. Tom comes home early from work and pries open the first crate with a crowbar. As the nails on the lid extract from the wood they make a loud, prolonged, screeching sound. Finally the nails are clear, and my dad removes the lid. The crate is packed right to the top with straw. Where are the packages? Where's my potato gun?

It's not straw. It's wood shaved into giant clusters like cotton candy. It was the standard packing material of the time. Very cheap, very efficient, and very inflammable, it was called Excelsior. My dad peeled the Excelsior back and started to uncover the treasures within. Anyone who has experienced the joy of a shipment will understand what fun this sudden potlatch was for everyone, and my little sisters got their polka-dot party dresses with matching hats.

So we're in the desert amidst some wooden crates spilling Excelsior all over, our natural impulse is to gather some of the shavings into a clump and light it on fire. Danny looks in his zippered pockets, I pat my jeans, and then Milt slips a matchbook out of his back pocket. We make a small pile of the stuff, and Milt opens the matchbook. There's only one match; when he strikes it, it bends in half. So he strikes the doubled-over match again with his thumb, and it flares up, stuck under his thumbnail. He screeches and shakes it off into the dirt. Oh well, we lose interest and wander farther into the desert.

Danny and Milt see a battered, rusted washing machine in the sand and head for it while I keep wandering toward the far fence. Oblivious, walking along, enjoying myself, I kneel to put my hand into a six-foot piece of ten-inch pipe half buried in the sand. I stretch my arm into the warm sand, raking my fingers to snag lizard eggs, when I hear, "You're under arrest."

I look up, and there is a kid with a gun pointed at me. He's an 8th grader, maybe a 9th grader, but I've never seen him before. With my arm half in the pipe, I say, "Arrest? Arrested for what?

Call him Cliff, a lean, handsome kid with alert eyes, a low brush-top haircut and a wide mouth with perfect teeth. His BB pistol is dead level with my chest; grimly, he nods over his left shoulder to a stack of bricks on a rise ten yards behind him. "Our hideout. You're trespassing on our fort. Get up." Like Clint Eastwood many years later, Cliff does grim with a grin. He's not really that serious. I throw up my hands, bite my thumbs, and say, "I surrender."

He says, "Why are you biting your thumbs?"

"My dad told me that was how Bedouin surrender to each other. They bite their thumbs."

"That's cool," says Cliff as he points the pistol at me and shouts, "Thumbs up!" which is actually pretty funny. We both laugh, he puts the pistol in his belt, motions me toward the fort, and tells me I don't have to bite my thumbs anymore. It's getting a little colder, so I zip up my coat. He pulls up the collar on his thin red windbreaker as a gust of wind passes.

Made of loosely stacked cinder blocks and roofed with strips of corrugated tin, the fort is about four feet high, four feet wide, and eight feet long with a crude gap in one wall for a door. As we approach the hideout, there's a shout, and Danny and Milt with their hands in the air trudge toward us in front of two guys I'll call Bugner and Eric.

Toting a Daisy BB rifle, Bugner is a slovenly middle-aged man trapped in a large 14-year-old's body. His smudged, thick glasses always out of kilter, he's clumsy and ungainly, but he is big—he weighs 30 pounds more than anyone else. Eric is an unfortunate combination of disparate DNA. He's a scrawny kid with white-blond, greased-back hair and pale eyebrows that are almost invisible. His hands and feet are too large for his age, and his languid, almost silver, eyes project a kind of malevolent stupidity. He's carrying a BB pistol that looks like a German Luger.

"Look what we found. Probably trying to sneak up on us," says Bugner as he pokes Milt in the back with his rifle.

"Sneaking up on you? Me and Danny were just trying to get the motor out of that washing machine. Sneaking up on what?" says Milt and then he sees the fort. "Hey, that's cool."

Eric replies, "See, Bugner! They were spying on us. There's only one way to deal with a spy." He points the 'Luger' at Milt's face and pronounces in a stern voice, "There's only one way: shoot him in the eye."

This seems a bit extreme. In the ensuing silence, I gulp, Danny cringes, and Milt covers his eyes with his hands. Cliff is speechless, but Bugner breaks out laughing, "Shoot him in the eye? Are you crazy? I'll shoot you in the butt."

Eric protests, "But..."

"You've got it right, right in your butt. Jeez, Eric ... Here's what we're going to do. They are going to march over there in front of the fort, and we're going to execute them for treason."

"Execute!" says Danny. "My brothers will beat you up."

"You'll be dead, so they'll never know," leers Eric.

The best retort I can come up with is that my mom will hound them to the ends of the earth as Bugner lines us up at the bottom of a gully in front of the fort. Cliff says, "We don't have blindfolds for them. You need blindfolds for an execution. Turn them around so they won't see our bullets."

So we're facing the desert, our backs to the firing squad about ten feet away. "Death to traitors," yells Eric as he fires a BB at Milt's back. The others open up, firing BBs into our backs. But we have on our heavy jackets, and Danny his leather one, so it doesn't hurt at all except for the missed shot that stings me in the calf, and I start hopping around.

"Are you hurt?" says Bugner. "You okay?"

"Yeah, I'm fine."

An exuberant Danny shouts out, "You can't hurt me! My leather jacket is bulletproof."

"Don't say that," whispers Milt, right before all the guns are directed at Danny. Every hit makes a satisfying, sharp pinging sound as it ricochets off the leather. Finally, Bugner says, "I'm out of ammo."

"So am I," says Eric.

"Didn't feel a thing. Not with this jacket," says Danny.

Cliff holsters his pistol and says, "Hey guys, you should see our fort."

"Yeah," says Bugner, "It's wicked. There were a bunch of cinder blocks, and we piled them up. Cliff found the tin strips over there. We put them over some 2-by-4s. We put some rocks on top so the wind won't blow the roof away. Don't you have an older sister in 9th grade?"

"Yeah, my sister Annie."

"I think my brother knows her.'

Eric scampers up to the fort, motions like a maître d', and says, "Gentlemen, please follow me," and ducks into the door. We crawl in after him. We have to duck walk since it's only four feet high, but once we sit in the dirt it's roomy enough. The cinder blocks do cut the wind, so it's warmer.

Otherwise it's empty, except for a giant heap of Excelsior right in the middle of the room.

Milt and I look at each other, "What?" But Bugner is telling an elaborate story about how he and his dad almost crashed into a dead donkey on the road to Dammam. We forget about the hay stack, as Danny tells us about the foot-long hooded viper that his dad accidentally backed over with his Buick. The viper was pointed lengthwise with the center of the tire, so it squashed him in a perfect line like a neck tie.

Eric and Danny are sitting across the pile of straw along the far side. Bugner is at the end and Cliff, Milt and I are along the wall closest to the door. Everyone is talking, and I'm wondering how did this happen. One minute, I'm being executed, now we're living it up as equals with these cool older guys. Oh, well.

Eric says, "Cliff, you got a cigarette?"

"Sure," and he throws him a cigarette.

I say, "Cliff, what's with the Excelsior?"

"It's for the winter. When it's real cold we'll pull off chunks and burn them in the corner. Bugner just thought of it. We haven't tried it yet."

"Cliff, do you have any matches?"

"Do you want me to smoke it for you, too?" replies Cliff. Milt and I have never heard this quip before, so we laugh out loud which brightens up Cliff, and he says, "Hey, Eric, want me to light it for you?"

Eric cracks a thin-lipped smile and replies, "You'd just light the filter and not know the difference. Watch how a pro does it. With one hand." He holds the matchbook up in his right hand and flicks open the cover to show us how it's done.

There is a reason that every matchbook since the dawn of man is printed with the warning: **Close Cover Before Striking**. Apparently Eric wasn't big for reading.

He says, "Watch this." And stretches his thumb to bend a match and run it along the sandpaper strip. The match head lights off fine. Too fine because it burns Eric's thumb. He pulls it back, which allows the match to flex back to its brethren. The whole matchbook goes up in flame, sulfur, and smoke. He tosses the fireball into the air, and it lands on his shirt. In his panic Eric bats it away.

All of us are frozen in place as we watch, in a sort of slow motion, the sizzling matchbook as it traces an arc directly into the Excelsior, which instantly explodes into a fireball. Two seconds later we're all racing out the door. Bugner stumbles and loses his glasses.

With his biker jacket hiked over his head, Danny barrels right over Bugner's back as he gropes around in the dirt for his lenses. Then a very dazed Eric stumbles out with his pomaded DA steaming, almost smoldering, but not quite on fire. There is the pungent scent of burning hair in the air. He slaps his head and smoothes his hair back with his hand, pretending that he had it all under control.

Dumbfounded into silence, we gather around the fort as it burns down in the desert just 300 yards east of 3rd Street. It's getting a little colder, the wind is picking up. The diffused sun is low in the sky.

For some reason, as if we'd just finished a Little League game, we all shake hands with each other before we drift away. When I shake hands with Eric I notice that his once pale, almost invisible eyebrows are neatly singed in place as if they were drawn by an expert with a thick eyebrow pencil.

Tim with a 30 pound *hamoor*

THE NIGHT OF THE HAMOOR

I'm fairly certain that there is no statute of limitations for crimes against humanity. I can only plead not guilty by reason of ignorance — and it seemed like the thing to do at the time. On second thought, it is much better to think of this story as entirely a work of fiction and any resemblance to anything that happened in Dhahran during the summer of 1964 is entirely coincidental.

His parents were out for a party, so Landis, Ben, and I gathered at Smith's house. His dad's air-conditioned den, built into the formerly screened-in patio, was a comfortable room with one of those skinny-legged, maple wood Hi-Fi cabinets. Smith was playing his lone Bo Diddley album with the bass cranked to ten. We were 16 years old, sophomore returning students. All of us went to male-only boarding schools, so whatever we once knew about social graces was eradicated, and we had not the slightest idea of how to talk to girls. Except for Landis. Somehow he was bilingual.

Our passion was spearfishing. At least four days a week, we were at the Dammam Pier, at Half Moon Bay, at the wonderful gap just south of Khobar where the Gulf ebbed and flowed into a compact bay. Quite illegally, we dove off the North Pier in Ras Tanura, where today you'd be shot on discovery. Snorkeling around, peering under countless underwater rock ledges searching for that tasty rock grouper, the *hamoor*. Every once in a while you'd be greeted by a sea snake as thick as a bicycle inner-tube boiling out of the hole straight at you.

Once Tommy H. happened to be using a trident spearhead instead of the usual single point, so he took a shot at a giant sea snake. He barely clipped it, and it attacked him so aggressively that he was desperately back-slashing at it with his fins, trying to fend it off. Before it could sink its fangs into his arm and inject him with its deadly poisonous venom, he managed to reload and get off a fatal shot. I saw the snake in his backyard in Dhahran. It was taller than him at six feet and as wide as a baseball bat.

For the four of us, snorkeling and spear-fishing were just about the highest form of art and friendship. Something that we all could do together, yet individually at the same time. And of course it gave us a common history as we shared our different adventures and travails in intricate detail. Braving the polluted waters off the Khobar Pier, dancing with porpoises in Half Moon Bay, trying to spear a skipjack ten feet away in open water. Grabbing one of those two-foot-long Rock sharks that idled in three feet of water near the shore at the Dammam pier. Holding it in your hands, the creature's strength and vitality are incredible. Falling into awe when a hundred-pound, green sea turtle paddles by at ten feet down. But most of the time just cruising along, mesmerized by the underwater world and hearing Jacques Cousteau in our heads.

So now we're in Smith's den listening to Bo explain to us: "You can't know a book by looking at its cover, and you can't judge a woman by looking at her mother." The beat goes on, when Smith says, "I shot a 35-pound *hamoor* yesterday."

This is the first any of us had heard, and we are instantly suspicious. Thirty-five pounds is a serious grouper, and any of us would have called everyone once we got back to camp. Landis says, "My ass, you got a 35-pound *hamoor*. You probably speared your hemorrhoid," which was pretty funny.

I say, "Where is it?"

Ben says, "Yeah, show us the fillets. Are they in your freezer?"

Smith's eyes twinkle behind his coke-bottle glasses and he cackles, "No. It's buried in the side yard."

Collectively, we say, "What?"

With an ear-to-ear smile across his broad face he tells us the story. He was diving on a favorite haunt, a derelict raft made of four oil barrels, a bunch of 2-by-4s, and a wooden deck that had sunk years ago in 20 feet of water about 30 yards from the Yacht Club pier. Apparently it was a primo habitat for *hamoor* because you could snag a good-sized *hamoor* one day, and the next day it would be replaced by another alpha *hamoor*.

Smith had made several dives on the raft when he spotted the big fish hidden in the shadows at the back of the raft. He surfaced, took a deep breath, and then swam down to claim his prize. He stealthily peeked under the raft's barnacled lip. The grouper was still there. He slipped his arbalette, a spear gun powered by rubber cords, under the raft and fired. There was no silt in the water. No struggle. The fish didn't even twitch. He was quite pleased because he had obviously delivered a clean kill – the rarely realized ideal of the true spear-fisher ethic.

He pulled at the spear to retrieve his fish, but it wouldn't come free. He pulled some more but ran out of breath. Reluctantly he abandoned his spear gun, which was still attached to the spear, and surfaced.

After a few minutes he dove down again. He grabbed the spear and started tugging and twisting at it. A minute later as he swam for air, he realized that the spear had embedded itself into a 2 by 4. He either had to free the spear from the raft or admit defeat and cut the line to his spear gun.

At 16 saving face is everything, so he spent more than an hour, diving down 20 feet every few minutes to struggle with the spear, trying to bend it back and forth for 90 seconds at a time before surfacing. Finally, after constantly worrying and working the shaft, he freed it. He had to leave it free to get another lungful of air and immediately submerged to claim victory. He retracted the mangled spear, bent in at least three places, and then the mighty *hamoor*. Triumphant, he rose from the depths and swam to shore with his trophy in tow.

At the beach he pulled off his mask and snorkel and examined the large grouper. It was actually about 26 pounds, but in his tiny reptilian brain he rounded it off to 35. He looked at its eyes and thought, *That's strange. It has cataracts.* Inspecting its gills, he noticed a light moss at the edges. He hefted it, and it wasn't pliable like a normal fish. It was fairly stiff. All of a sudden, a flashbulb went off in the deep recesses of the tiny ganglia that operated his brain: he realized that the instant before he pulled the trigger the *hamoor* seemed to be swimming upside down. He had speared a dead *hamoor*.

By the time Smith finished his story we were all weeping from laughter. And in a strange way, Smith probably enjoyed making us dissolve into hysterics as much as he would have gloried over spearing a five-foot-long barracuda in open water. Life is very good. Bo is telling us that he wears a cobra skin for a neck tie, when Landis says, "So it wasn't 35 pounds?"

Smith recoils in innocence, "At least. I wouldn't kid you. I can prove it."

So for some totally inexplicable reason all four of us leave the air conditioned den with Bo Diddley and ice-cold Tuborg ginger ale to cluster on a very humid August night in the side yard as Smith excavates the 35-pound grouper that he buried yesterday. He uncovers the corpse, and we are knocked over by the atomic bomb of smell warfare. Smith has a head cold, but we're dying. He clears the dirt off and says, "Thirty-five pounds, easy."

Defying his gag reflex, Landis says, "No way. Maybe 25."

At this point Smith is a little bit giddy and replies, "No honest. I'll prove it to you." And he reaches down, grabs the *hamoor* by its eye sockets, and lifts it out of its grave.

"See. Look how long it is. At least 32 pounds," he says with a grin as he holds it up to chest level. Ten seconds later the pustulent-green, decayed tail fin slips off the fish back to the ground, and it is considerably shorter.

"There goes three pounds," says Landis. This is absolutely hilarious.

By the standards of any civilized society from the most remote village in New Guinea to downtown Copenhagen, any vaguely normal person would re-bury the fish and move on in life. But not us. Simultaneously, we decide that the best possible thing to do is to aimlessly carry this rotting *hamoor* through the streets of Dhahran.

We go into the alley and head to 8th Street. It's a fairly broad street; we're on one side, and Smith with the fish is on the other, and we can barely stand the odor. At one point, the fish slips and touches one of his tennis shoes. Subsequently, this shoe will have to be burned.

Cracking each other up with wise-ass commentary, we naturally, and unintentionally, drift towards recreation until we come to the infamous intersection of Hoover Street, the road straight down from recreation, and 8th Street. On the southwest corner is the empty house of the recently retired Dr. Brown, who delivered half of us and was a legendary figure in Aramco medicine. On the opposite side is a venerable, brick seven-unit apartment shaped in a U that has been there forever.

It wasn't really our fault. We never had any plan or intentions. We were just walking around with a dead fish.

However, when we rounded the corner and saw the seven-unit, we instantly had the same inspiration and didn't need to say a word. Five minutes later, around ten o'clock on a weekday night, Smith, the fish, and I are in the always-unlocked AC room at the rear of the apartments. I lift out the AC unit's heavy, steel air filter, Smith drops in the *hamoor*, I replace the filter, and we are gone like the breeze.

The four of us sprint across Hoover into the alley behind Dr. Brown's, enter through the back gate, and make our way to the front yard to watch the apartments through the hedge.

"Nothing is happening."

"Not a thing."

"Wait. A light went on in that window."

"Someone is walking through the kitchen."

"There's a light in that apartment."

Suddenly, all the lights of the building go on like an overloaded switchboard. Crouched behind the hedge, we are dying — not from laughter, but from trying to stifle it, so we don't reveal our hiding place.

Then a porch light directly across from us blinks on. A lean, gray-haired guy wearing a bathrobe opens the door and leans his head out. Like a hunting dog he takes a couple of deep sniffs, and we completely lose it. Rolling in convulsions on Dr. Brown's lawn. We take another peek, and now all the back doors are opening. This is hilariously funny, like watching a Buster Keaton movie in real time, but our survival demands that we make ourselves scarce, so we flee down the alley away from the apartments.

We are completely stoked. Our brilliant insight is that if we circle around to recreation and then innocently happen to be walking down Hoover to 8th, we can check out the chaos. It takes us about six minutes. There are already a dozen adults on the corner. No one pays any attention to us because the fire truck rolls up to join a dozen trucks and cars clustered on the curb.

In the courtyard in front of the building the residents are shuffling around in a daze talking to each other. There's the grizzled night foreman, Burt Simmons. Bricklin, the head of security, has a half-dozen of his Saudi patrolman standing around. A black sedan pulls up, and Quint Tocksin, the District Manager, steps out of the car.

Lean and tall, he's resplendent in a white linen suit, highly-polished, black Italian loafers, his thick wavy hair carefully pomaded. There is a cloud of dark fury floating above his head. He has been at a state dinner with the governor of the province and the visiting president of Standard Oil of California – and now he is a plumber responding to a service call for a backed-up toilet. He told Burt that on the phone; however, the night foreman had 30 years of experience in oil camps from Indonesia to Peru. Burt said, "But Quint, what if this is the canary in the coal mine? It could be a helluva lot worse. Some damn thing that's leaking hydrogen sulfide gas into the system. It smells damn awful, not like rotting eggs but something even worse. It could kill half a dozen people."

Quint really, really wants this to be a fouled sewer pipe, so he can hop in his Buick and get back to the banquet. As the crowd recognizes him, he straightens his posture. Even though he has no idea what is going on, he dons the confident face of the manager who has seen everything before.

He walks straight up to the refugees clustered on the lawn courtyard in front of their apartments. Greets by name the people he knows and nods to the others. He really doesn't want to hear about their trauma, so he immediately says how sorry he is for their plight. We'll take care of it right away. It's probably just a backed-up sewer pipe. He would have given them all free drinks coupons if he had them.

He's rescued when the bow-legged Burt Simmons ambles over for a private conversation.

"Where is this smell coming from?" says Quint.

"It's everywhere. Bricklin's guys are trying to pinpoint it."

"It doesn't smell too bad."

"Not until you get closer."

"Oh, hell. It's just a clogged toilet."

"The worst one I ever smelled."

"I'm going to go into that corner apartment, walk around, take a whiff, and prove it."

"No, you don't want to do that."

"Watch me," and with all the casualness he can muster Quint walks to Apartment Three.

Meanwhile, Bricklin and Hatim, the sergeant of the Saudi patrolmen, wearing Scott air masks like the firemen use, exit from the back door of Apartment Two – the same porch-door that guy in the bathrobe used. We're starting to inflate at the cheeks from repressed laughter, when one of the bystanders on the corner says, "What's that smell?" and looks at Smith.

I look down at the steaming fish-goo on his tennis shoe and quickly say, "Oh, it must be a breeze from the apartments," as I nudge Smith off the corner and downwind across the street.

Bricklin and Hatim go to the back of the yard fronting Hoover Street, take off their masks, and start talking. Bricklin is sure that he is missing a clue or forgetting to do something vital. It's good to get that mask off, and he'll spend a minute or two in the night air to think about it. Hatim lights up a Salem cigarette.

Fritz Adrian was a brilliant cartographer, responsible for many of the finest maps Aramco ever produced. His wife Stella was a tiny, bright-eyed Austrian woman with endless energy. An accomplished harpist who could play jazz clarinet. They were eligible for upgraded housing but liked their apartment. Apartment Three.

Most of the lights in all of the apartments are on as Quint approaches the Adrians'. The blinds are open, and it looks like a diorama that Fritz and Stella have just stepped out of for a minute. The front door is wide open. He gets about ten feet away before the wall of stench stops him like an invisible force field.

He pauses and pretends he is carefully inspecting the place as he thinks to himself, "It doesn't smell like bad eggs, so it's not hydrogen sulfide. This is a terrible stink. Oh well, I can hold my breath for a minute. I'll take a big breath, go in the door, walk around for a moment, and then stroll out like everything is fine. Then leave."

He walks into the Adrians' tidy, almost minimalist living room – a couch, two easy chairs, and a coffee table. The walls tastefully decorated with Fritz's collection of antique maps and tapestries woven by Bedouin women whom Stella knew. The carpet is an understated, light slate color that sets off the furnishings quite nicely.

Off the living room, near the hallway to the back of the apartment, stands Stella's harp. A tall gilt-covered beauty carved with vines and leaves galore. The half-naked angel at the top of the instrument had caused a big uproar at customs. It was bad enough that the harp was a musical instrument, but this sculpture of a wanton angel was the last straw. Customs had impounded it and denied clearance.

The next day Stella called an Aramco taxi cab. At this time the security at Dammam customs was fairly decent. Not just anyone could come barging in, but there was no protocol to deal with an angry, five-foot-tall Austrian woman. Stella sliced right past two soldiers with fixed bayonets, a policeman with a revolver, a handful of clerks, and a panicked Hijazi office manager who followed behind her as she burst into the Director-General of Customs' office.

Fadl, the Director-General, has just concluded an arrangement with Najib, the Lebanese representative of Middle East Airlines, and Khalil, their Saudi agent, and is having a cup of tea with them when Stella appears, screaming in German-accentuated English for about a minute before concluding with the words, "I want my harp."

The room goes dead silent. Fadl speaks very little English and has no idea who this woman is. He asks Najib in Arabic, "What is she talking about?"

"She wants her harp," replies Najib.

The Director-General stares coldly at Stella for half a minute and then starts laughing. Except for her blonde hair, she looks exactly like his diminutive wife Fawzia on a bad day. And Stella got her harp back.

Quint has now spent 20 seconds in the living room. Aware that he can be seen from the courtyard, he figures that he'll slip out of sight into the hallway, wait 20 seconds, and then casually walk out of the apartment. Even though he's not breathing, the stench is attacking his nostrils. Once out of sight he clamps his fingers over his nose.

In the backyard, Hatim has barely smoked half of his Salem when it suddenly occurs to Bricklin that maybe it is a gas leak. "Hatim, put that out. We have to turn off the electricity right now. The whole place could blow up," as he scrambles to the power box at the back of the building.

In the hallway, Quint counts patiently, "Eighteen, nineteen, twenty seconds. I'm out of here." He turns to leave, and the lights go out. What! He spins around. He steps forward right into a wall. He's confused, sees the faint glow of the street lights through the living room windows, and rushes forward. He takes two steps and then trips at the end of the hallway, throws out his right arm to cushion the fall and plunges straight into the harp. His hand goes straight through the harp's strings as it falls to the floor with a loud discordant noise.

The fall knocks the air out of him, he gasps, he inhales, and then it's over. At first he gags, then everything he has eaten for the last week comes surging forth. His right arm is pinned beneath the harp. With his left hand he claws at his tie and rips the two top buttons off his shirt trying to breath, but the next breath is just as bad as the first one. Finally he extracts his arm from the harp. Every knuckle of his hand is bleeding profusely over the Adrians' carpet as he manages to stand up and stumble out of Apartment Three.

His face is a pale green, his eyes albino pink, his hair is matted in sweat over his brow, and his right arm is trailing a bloody hand that he wipes off on the leg of his white linen trousers. His finely tailored dinner jacket is a science experiment in stomach bile and various ingredients. Quint manages about ten feet before he skids to his knees on the courtyard lawn.

Burt is standing there with a thermos of coffee. "That didn't work out so well. Here, drink this," and hands him a cup. Quint snatches it like a slightly demented beggar, drains it in two giant gulps, and composes himself. After a few moments he stands up, ready to pretend that everything is fine. The newly acquired deep-green grass stains on each knee of his dress whites don't do much to abet that pretense.

Burt says, "What the hell?"

"What the hell? What happened to the lights?"

"I'm not sure. All of a sudden they went out."

Before Quint can say another word, Bricklin comes trotting up like a needy German shepherd looking for a milk bone and a pat on the head.

"Lucky I realized that the whole place might blow up and cut the electricity."

Quint focuses his eyes in pure hatred at Bricklin and smolders — while reminding himself that Bricklin's performance review is coming up next month. Burt says, "What? Why didn't you clear it with me?'

"There was no time. It was do or die."

"Die," thinks Quint as he wipes his face clean with his filthy, bloody sleeve.

Burt says, "Did you find the source? What is it?

"Hatim discovered the problem. It's kids."

"Kids?" croaks Quint. "What's kids?"

"We don't know who. But someone put a dead *hamoor* in the AC unit."

"Yup," says Burt, "only kids would do something like that."

Quint stares through his pink-shot eyes at Burt. Looks over at the group of displaced residents. Oh my God, there's Stella Adrian. She's smiling and waving at him. Quickly he turns to Burt and says, "Fix it." And then confidently strides across the lawn directly to his Buick.

His shirt is ripped at the neck, and his white linen dress suit is permanently stained with gastric acid, blood, and Bermuda grass. He believes he can still pull this off when on his third step he realizes that he has lost his right shoe in the apartment. He runs the rest of the way to his sedan and drives off.

Burt Simmons turns to Bricklin, "Fix it."

Bricklin turns to Hatim, "Fix it."

Hatim turns to Issa, his second in command, and says, "Fix it."

Issa spots 19-year-old Ali, who is new on the job, and says, "Fix it."

Somehow, young Ali finds an old Omani gardener sleeping under a bower of oleanders and says, "Fix it."

There aren't many people left on the corner still watching. Smith and Landis have departed to go burn his tennis shoe, and Ben has faded away in the hope that Jeannie might still be up. The refugees have all left to spend the night with friends, but there are still about twenty salaried Aramco employees hanging around – half a dozen Americans and the rest Saudi firemen and security guys.

I move up from the corner to the alley on the other side of the street and see Ali leading the Omani gardener to the AC room. He looks in and then, completely oblivious to everyone watching, crosses the alley to root around in a garbage can until he finds a brown paper bag. Apparently, the deal is that he gets to keep the *hamoor*.

The gardener steps into the AC room for a minute and then comes out with the paper sack in his arms. Watching from across the street, it's pretty funny to see everyone part like the Red Sea. The invisible stink from the dripping bag presses them all against the side fences as the old man blithely trots through them, down the alley, and down Hoover street.

That night back in his lair, the old gardener thinks to himself, *Tomorrow, I'll go to that mimsahb's house on 6th Street where I planted those hibiscuses last week. She's tall and beautiful for an American — though way too skinny, but she's cheerful and always greets me kindly. More than once she sends her servant out to bring me an ice-cold bottle of Tuborg ginger ale. I'll cut the fish up and bury it all around those flowers, and they'll please her.*

Her husky son with the thick glasses is okay, too. Several times this summer, he's given me fresh hamoor heads from his catch. He's so generous. Too generous. It's as if he doesn't know that the cheeks are the best part.

SPUNKY

After six years in the States, where I worked in movies and television production, in January of 1974 I returned to Arabia to start up the television department at the King Faisal Specialist Hospital in Riyadh. I was one of the first 20 American employees, and the hospital was still being built when I arrived. Housing was tight, so I lived with my brother Michael, who had already been there for two years living in a compound of three villas – actually spacious, one-story bungalows, surrounded by the usual, God-awful cinderblock wall facing the street.

Michael worked for Citibank as an account executive; one of the perks was they'd finance any car he wanted, so he bought a new burgundy Pontiac Bonneville with one of those vinyl landau roofs that were so popular then. It was a sweet ride, comfy seats, dynamite air conditioning, and a killer built-in 8-track with surround speakers. Unfortunately, it was low to the ground with soft suspension. Great on the strip in LA, but the mean streets of Riyadh immediately chewed up that Pontiac. I doubt if that car ever had all four wheels properly aligned since it left Detroit.

In the first few years after the 1973 oil boom, hundreds of European and American technocrats, construction superintendents, management experts, and outright speculators had come and gone. An odd consequence of this phenomenon was that many of them left their dogs behind. I went to the Riyadh Zoo in 1974, and one of the enclosures displayed a pair of Great Danes, the present of some departing Scandinavian dignitary. So, I'm more than willing to believe the legend of the Dog Gang known to all in the expatriate community.

In those early days, these high-level consultants and managers, their families — and their dogs — would fly into Riyadh, only to be removed or replaced for a variety of reasons within a year or so. Sometimes it was just easier to turn Fido over to the gardener and give him 100 riyals. The Swiss broker in a failed bauxite mega-deal just ejected his tiresome Dalmatian into the alley and flew to Zurich. But of course too, there was seven-year-old Lucy. Just two hours before she and her family left for the airport, Spunky, her dear dachshund companion, "escaped from the yard." She waited and waited for him to come back, until the family had to drive off from their villa to the airport. Lucy crying for Spunky and pounding against the rear window the whole way.

The foreign breeds were not accepted by the resident packs of feral dogs. Actually, it was quite dangerous for the Yorkies and Pomerians of this world. Eventually, a German shepherd met a wild, unshorn standard poodle abandoned by a Belgian bond trader. They encountered a sheltie and a bulldog. Soon an Irish setter, a golden labrador, two terriers, and a lazy, old cocker spaniel joined up. They careened around the outskirts of Riyadh, scraping along as best as they could, learning that food didn't come in cans anymore, until one day they met their alpha male. And the Expat Dog Gang began its reign of terror.

It's about five in the morning. The air is damp and cool, a soft ground haze hovers just before the dawn. The dogs are silently slinking along both sides of the dark street. The cocker spaniel gets distracted by a cat's hairball and trails behind. Their victim is in sight, but they can't afford to be careless, so they sneak closer. Waiting for the signal.

They are about five yards from the prey when there is a sharp, "Yip, Yip," and Spunky leads the attack on my brother's burgundy Bonneville. He leaps up to the bumper - twice, scrambles over the trunk like an uncoiled Slinky, and mounts the landau roof. The feral dachshund emits a wild, spine-tightening howl and then slashes the vinyl with his claws. Seconds later the entire pack, terriers and all, is crowded on to the top of my brother's car slicing the faux Corinthian leather into ribbons.

By some entirely unanticipated design flaw, the vinyl top was bonded to the entire surface of the inner steel with an organic-based glue probably made from rendered race horses, but secured around the perimeter with fancy trim. Mother Nature will always find a way. It turned out that the glue area between the vinyl and the steel, a thin layer subjected to fantastic temperature extremes in the Arabian sun, bubbled up and just happened to provide an ideal feeding ground for a species of grub that was full of protein and apparently quite tasty.

The dog pack shredded off long burgundy strips and licked the steel roof clean, as if they were crazed socialites at an all-you-can-eat caviar buffet. Spunky saw headlights down the block, growled twice, and the pack evaporated into the shadows.

As the dogs faded off, just as the sun rose to thrust a low-lying stab of light down the street, Spunky returned to stand 20 yards away, casting a long shadow on his victim. He yipped twice at the violated Pontiac. Barked to himself a soft congratulations, and then waddled off to join his gang.

Two hours later, my brother, who is fluent in many languages, comes out of his villa, opens the gate to the street and begins swearing in a bewildering string of obscenities ranging from traditional Anglo-Saxon to colorful Arabic words and off into allusions to Zoroastrian deities. Worn out, he calls the office to say he wouldn't be in and listens to Wagner playing loudly on his Hi-Fi long into the night.

Central Riyadh - *David Hills 1976*

DRIVING RIYADH

In the mid-1970s if there had been an institution of higher learning such as Harvard, Oxford, or the Sorbonne that hosted an advanced degree in Automotive Survival there is little doubt that doctorates would have required not only a learned thesis, but also a 90-day residency in Riyadh, Saudi Arabia – a hands-on tutorial in a turbulent driving environment that was part pinball machine, part bumper cars, and always a game of cat and mouse.

With the sudden wealth that came with the oil price hikes in 1973, the country went on a car-buying binge. Motor vehicle sales exploded; the volume of cars imported doubled every three months. The demand was so great that Honest Ali of Manfuhah was smuggling in dozens of beat-up cars a week from Kuwait. Lebanese teenagers could pool their money, hitchhike to Germany to buy a used Mercedes, and drive it to Jeddah to triple their investment and have a spectacular adventure in the process. The problem was that there were many more cars than there were halfway competent drivers. To make matters worse, very few even had a driver's license, and the rest didn't care and drove like madmen.

In early 1974, I was one of the first Americans to staff the new King Faisal Specialist Hospital in Riyadh – though it was still being built. So when I went for my driver's license, I had the chance to closely examine the Riyadh Department of Motor Vehicles, located in a broad post-Ottoman-style, late 1940s building fronted by a wide, pillared portico that lured you in by its shade. I arrived with Clem, a retired US Navy electronics specialist who managed the hospital's electronics equipment.

We walked through a battered, wide double-door into a large room, that had only been painted once 40 years ago, filled with babbling, excitable voices and hundreds of Saudis and Yemenis, Sudanese, Syrians, Pakistanis — you name it — all trying to get to the front counter spanning the opposite wall. Before he conveniently disappeared, our agent did manage to fill out our license applications and usher us into the optical exam room without too much delay. While we're waiting Clem says, "You know I'm blind in one eye?"

"No, I didn't know that."

"Well, watch me ace this test."

"What…" and then I was called to read the eye chart. I read down the list far enough and the examiner, a cheerful, barely 20-year-old signed me off. Then Clem sat down.

The kid asked Clem to cover his left eye and read the chart. Clem brought up his left hand over his eye and read the chart. The examiner asked him to cover his other eye, and Clem brought up his right hand and placed it over his left eye - the same eye. He read the chart and was on his way.

I was amazed at this psychological trick. "Clem, that was really something."

With a wide grin, he said, "If it worked for twenty years in the US Navy, why not here?"

I filed this item in my special techniques database in the sub-folder marked "Misdirection" and prepped myself for show time. We returned to the main hall which now seemed to teem with even more men waiting to approach the counter. At least ten guys deep.

Londoners are famous for their queues, patiently waiting in a tidy line for the bus. Middle Easterners take a different approach and use the horizontal queue to mob the counter, screaming and waving forms in the air, trying desperately to get one of the half-dozen officials to pay attention.

The clerks are middle-aged Saudis in *thobes* and *ghuttras*, but by some miraculous life force are cut from the same cloth as DMV employees in San Diego, Paris, or Istanbul. They begin their day bored to death, and it only goes downhill from there. It would be a great job if they never had to meet the public.

The horizontal line method sort of works; eventually, people clear out, and you can advance a step closer. However, you are standing in close quarters, so you must never step back or leave an opening between you and the fellow next to you, lest someone else slip through.

So I'm literally pressed shoulder to shoulder with Saudis on either side. I make some very small talk in my elementary Arabic, and they are cordial. In the rows in front of us everyone is also tightly squeezed. Ahead at the counter, a scowling, very short Saudi about 30 years old is trying to leave directly through the rest of us packed together in a virtual sardine can.

Finally, Shorty makes it to the row just ahead of me, but no one wants to step aside so he can get through. It'd be easy to lose your place. Eventually, he literally pries two guys apart enough to pass and steps through them. Almost instantly they close up, shoulder to shoulder, and catch the end of Shorty's *ghuttra* between them.

He takes another half-step before his head snaps back, and he falls to the floor. I don't think that I've ever heard so many men from so many different places, speaking such a wild range of languages and dialects, laugh so hard at the same time. It was so contagious that even guys who hadn't witnessed Shorty's pratfall were laughing.

The rest of the process wasn't too bad. There is a bizarre etiquette involved in the horizontal method. As you approach the counter, you wave your application in the air and shout. As you get closer, you keep waving but try to make eye contact and be empathetic, as if you cared about the clerk as a person. If you are Lebanese, you whisper to the official that he is so handsome that it is impossible that he is not a leading man in Egyptian cinema.

It sounds more or less orderly, but there is a wild card. As slow as they are, the clerks do take some pleasure from being in demand. They take the closest application, even if it's from some guy stretching from the second row; they banter with applicants and have that uncanny ability — like waiters in certain expensive restaurants — to walk through the dining room without seeing that the neglected Donner party of four at table nine has resorted to cannibalism.

So they ignore the earnest besetments from a fellow like Shorty and amuse themselves with the tall, willowy Somali with filed teeth or the fifteen-year-old Bedouin kid who will take his license and get his first job driving a Mercedes dump truck loaded with granite boulders through the heart of the city at rush hour.

This all worked in my favor. Being so tall I might as well have been the only American in the hall. Clem, about the size of an average Yemeni, was lost somewhere behind me. A great novelty at the DMV, I was a foot taller than almost everyone in the room. I could say, "*Hina! Hina!* Here! Here!" as well as anyone else and wave my papers nine feet in the air. By the time I got to the third row, one of the clerks was waiting and, with a big smile, waved me on. I stretched over two men to deliver my application. He stamped it, and I was on my way into the then-world's capital of vehicular injury and misery known as the streets of Riyadh.

The highways that connected the city to the rest of the kingdom and the few boulevards, many of them freshly built on the outskirts, were about the only place where a driver could gain enough velocity to totally demolish his vehicle. There were few, but horrendous, accidents.

However, within Riyadh, at the traffic circles, at the stop lights, down in the old city was where the struggle was fiercest. Saudi drivers somehow decided that a two-lane road was actually meant for three cars abreast. Cab drivers and Bedouin considered a traffic light optional — and sometimes one-way streets, too. One morning in central Riyadh, my brother saw an old Bedu in a battered Datsun pickup truck harangue a police car into backing up, as he drove the wrong way down a narrow street shouting, "*Haggi!* My right!" all the way.

Idling at an intersection one very warm afternoon, I realized that I was surrounded by physicists capable of calculating in real time that mass times acceleration equals force and ceding the right of way to the largest number. So our fifteen-year-old Bedouin kid with his new driver's license, barreling down Batha Street with a dump truck load of paving stones, had carte blanche at the next stop sign.

That's an obvious example, but a more nuanced, desperate game was played between delivery vans and pickup trucks, Pontiacs and Peugeots, Suzukis and Fiats. Traffic circles resembled the chariot scenes from *Ben Hur* on lots of caffeine. The swarms of cheap motorbikes had no right of way – ever, and survived as best they could, sometimes drafting behind the giant freight trucks and fuel tankers like remoras.

I was lucky because I had started driving in the minor-league city of Al Khobar before I was called up to the majors. First in Riyadh, and then Jeddah, I learned the most fundamental truth about driving in Arabia, the US, or anywhere else: they are all trying to kill you. And they believe the same about yours truly. Once that is realized, it does wonders for your driving awareness. Eventually, you understand that in dense urban traffic there are threats from all directions, so the best you can do is focus ahead, watch the width of your front fenders, try not to smash into anybody, and abandon the side doors and the rear of your car to fate.

I had a great job at the hospital, setting up its TV studio, programming the hospital's three-channel closed-circuit TV network, and organizing the operating-room cameras into a smaller studio solely devoted to filming surgical procedures. But the real reason I was in Riyadh was to drive around Arabia. With my driver's license in hand I set out to buy a vehicle that would get me there.

A car was pretty much out of the equation. It would take me around the city conveniently enough, but the older streets could be suddenly treacherous. There was a stealth pothole near the Al-Yammah Hotel that claimed dozens of front-end alignments a day. I wanted to drive into the desert anyway.

There were a lot of pickup trucks available, though the Japanese models were too compact for me, and I wanted a backseat. The vehicles closest to what we now call a SUV were the Chevy Blazer and the Toyota Land Cruiser, but they were new and pricey. I was in the back of a cab going to the hospital when I heard the sound of big tires. I looked back to see destiny rolling up on my right.

The jeep parked at Gerrin Village in Riyadh -1974

DRIVING RIYADH ~ THE BEAST

It was as big as a full-size American pickup truck, but configured like a van so the driver rode above the front wheels with no hood in the way. The huge tires provided lots of ground clearance and hummed hypnotically as the Beast drove past.

I later learned that it was a Volvo Laplander jeep with a canvas top especially configured for the Saudi National Guard. Sweden sold 600 of them to Saudi Arabia in a late 1960s arms deal. Actually much bigger than a Jeep, the Laplander was an eight-man troop carrier. It was the perfect desert vehicle, the proto Hummer 20 years before its time. Unfortunately, all the Laplanders were owned by the Saudi Arabian National Guard.

In the next few weeks I became aware of all the National Guard Volvos running around the city, and I was helplessly enamored. I had to have one, but where could I find one for sale? I asked around the hospital. I talked to the Saudi in charge of whisking arriving Americans through immigration and customs, to the skinny, sharp-dressed Eritrean who worked in local purchasing and knew half of the merchants in Riyadh, and I asked Antar, the huge, always-smiling, Sudanese heavy-truck driver whom I met while producing a training video on proper forklift techniques; they all agreed that I needed to go to the *Suq al-sayaraat mustamaal* – the used car suq. So one day I flagged down a cab and asked him to take me to one of the most astonishing places in all of Saudi Arabia.

Located on the eastern edge of town, the *suq* was bordered on one side with at least a dozen coffee houses and thatched-roof restaurants and a row of shabby car parts stores in cheaply built cinderblock stalls. It faced a huge lot, about half a football field in size, dotted with four-foot-high molehills. Ali bin Trump, or whoever was the landlord, had built them by having a dump truck drop a load of dirt and then spraying it with heavy tar. A few days in the sun, and the tar formed a hard crust that kept the mound in place.

The ground was littered with a fine layer of tiny beads of broken glass and colored plastic, nuts, bolts, varicolored wire, flattened juice cans, and the like pressed into the good earth which was stained with a range of automotive liquids from brake and transmission fluid to gobs of grease, gasoline, and diesel fuel which breathed a sweet bouquet of hydrocarbons into the air.

As the cab approached I began to hear a muffled roar. The closer I got, the louder the din became. Finally I emerged from the taxi to behold the most amazing spectacle. There were more than a thousand men milling around, the air was thick with exhaust fumes and burning rubber, the sound of dozens of revved engines, screeching tires, and squalling brakes combined to create a symphony of anarchy. The screams and shouts of scores of men standing atop mole hills with portable PA systems and the strangled responses from the customers provided the chorus of chaos.

I was dazed by the energy of the place, by the hundreds of cars on the perimeter waiting for their chance in the arena, by tea boys scurrying out with their full trays, and most of all by the sheer diversity of men and vehicles. Half of the crowd were Saudis, the rest Arabs from Iraq to Yemen, Africans, and Asians — all of them car guys! I could have been at a used car auction in Paducah, Kentucky, minus the chaw, Jack Daniels, and country music. Everyone was either talking or smoking or doing both. And the cars were from just about every model of vehicle ever made outside the Soviet Bloc.

I wandered over to the nearest auction to see what was happening. Standing on his mound, a husky Syrian with a rich bass voice and rapid-fire delivery was extolling the virtues of an abused Datsun pickup truck. Standing to one side at the base of the mound the twitchy Saudi car dealer monitored his mouthpiece.

The Syrian finished his spiel and waved to the teenaged Yemeni driver who popped the clutch in reverse and shot 15 feet backwards before slamming on the brakes. He revved the engine and then spat forward, screeching to a halt just before the mound. He laid into the horn to demonstrate that most vital component. He did this repeatedly as the auctioneer raised the bid to past a thousand riyals. The kid came blasting forward again, slammed the Datsun into reverse, let go of the clutch, and there was a loud clunk. He desperately shifted, revved the engine, but the truck just sat there making a chunky sound from the transmission that only added to the ambient cacophony.

The kid desperately pounded the clutch and pumped the gas, the Syrian screamed at the kid, and the Saudi car dealer harangued the auctioneer as the crowd drifted away. But no matter, there were dozens of auctions going on, each one an individual tableau of auto commerce, Saudi style. After a while I realized that they were selling cars the same way they once sold camels, though you didn't have to examine the teeth and pull out the tongue for careful inspection.

Eventually, I encountered a mound mounted by a diminutive, mid-50s Saudi, clean-shaven, in a snow-white *thobe* and no PA system. I'll call him Abu Ali. A late-model Cadillac was being driven away by some Yemeni teenager, while his younger cousin maneuvered in a sky-blue, 1973 Chrysler Imperial Lebaron to a collective sigh of approval from the gallery — a much more upscale crowd with lots of young Saudi men in clean *thobes* and *ghuttras* perfectly folded into whatever was the snappy style of the moment and Jordanian business men in pressed suits. But of course there was a big crowd of looky-loos: toothless Bedu with nothing else to do, Indian clerks, Baluchi mechanics, and lots of guys wandering around aimlessly, lured by the sleek Imperial – like myself.

Once the kid parked the car with the engine running, he hopped out of the car, and seemingly out of nowhere, the demo driver appeared. A very tall Kenyan, maybe even a Masai, maybe named Musa, was dressed from his polished Italian loafers and tan linen pants up to his starched white shirt with French collars attached by red stone cuff links. He slipped into the car like slow mercury and closed the door.

He tapped the gas lightly, slid back the seat, adjusted its tilt angle - it had remote-control mirrors, so he wiggled them back and forth to set them just right. Normally, by now the crowd would be screaming and shouting to get the auction started, but everyone got quieter as Musa flipped on the headlights and blinked them high and low. Flicked on the turn signals, then the hazard lights and lowered and raised each of the power windows. Then he leaned forward to the dashboard, put the AC at max, and tuned into a station on the radio. We could barely hear it until he dropped the driver's window — you could almost feel the AC pouring out — and turned up the volume on some soulful Oud music.

Musa had a long, mute face, a handsome profile worthy of a fine work of sculpture, a slight grin emerged at the corners of his mouth as he slipped the Imperial into gear, and without a sound, the huge vehicle glided to the mound and gently pulled to a stop. Finally, Abu Ali started speaking in a surprisingly deep voice — it was much deeper than he was tall. I didn't know that much Arabic but enough to figure out that he was telling us that this cream puff was owned by a little old man who hardly used it. It had 5,000 miles on it and was only one year old. It was a beautiful shade of blue tastefully set off with a lot of chrome. As he progressed, he lowered his voice; everyone became quieter and leaned closer. How could anyone not want this car? And then he signaled to Musa.

Musa redlined the engine and let it scream, slammed the Lebaron into reverse, and the car shot back thirty feet in three seconds and stopped instantly. Musa changed the station to some wild Turkish music and then very slowly drove forward, shimmying the wheels back and forth to make the car undulate like a python. We were mesmerized and hushed as Abu Ali extolled all the Chrysler's options while Musa demonstrated them. For the part about the crimson red leather interior, Musa opened the driver's door to show off the Naugahyde. When he finished, Musa quietly backed up the Imperial and then began slowly going back and forth to the mound as if the car were a cloud.

Abu Ali said, "Do I hear 10,000 riyals?" Which was immediately countered, and the price of the Chrysler started to climb. Now, I don't have any idea of what a brand new Chrysler Imperial actually cost in those days, so I'll arbitrarily say 50,000 riyals (about $13,000). Well the price quickly hit 40,000. I noticed that there was a young, handsome Saudi with a pencil-thin mustache and three twenty-something friends also from equally wealthy families bidding against a portly Egyptian with a sweaty brow in a rumpled tan suit and an elderly Indonesian gentleman in a neat, white shirt with epaulettes wearing Sukarno sunglasses. The rest of us hoi polloi crowded around to watch the duel.

The Indonesian dropped out at 45,000 riyals, and the other two raised the price to 49,000 – almost the price for a brand-new Chrysler, but you'd have to wait four months for delivery. Finally the young Saudi had the top bid at

50,000, and the Egyptian quit. As all auctioneers do, Abu Ali searched the crowd and started the countdown which is apparently the tradition everywhere on earth. "Going once, going twice, ..." and then I heard a nearby voice say, "Fifty-five thousand."

The young Saudi blanched, and I turned to see a weathered Yemeni in filthy overalls, work boots and an electrician's work belt waving a fistful of 100 riyal bills in his hand. His face was partially scarred with smallpox; he had a wide smile that revealed three gold front teeth and the rest rusted with a combination of cigarettes, betel nut and tooth decay. I'll call him Yayha because later in Jeddah I knew a Yemeni much like him.

The life of a Yemeni electrician was quite perilous, about a third of them being inadvertently electrocuted in their first week on the job. Blissfully unaware of Ohm's law or Von Helmholtz's first theorem, they pressed on: connecting red wires to red wires and learning the perils of grounding yourself to a high-voltage line while standing in water. I imagined that the energetic Yayha was rolling in riyals because he was the electrical contractor of choice in the poorer neighborhoods of Riyadh. Rapid expansion had stressed the municipality beyond its limits, and service to these older areas was virtually ignored, so Yayha would climb a pole, tap into a live high-voltage line, string dozens of illegal power lines down the street, and bill his customers monthly.

Abu Ali repeated, "Fifty-five thousand." The young Saudi turned to his pals, who half-heartedly patted their pockets and gazed at the sky. It soon became obvious that he didn't have 56,000 riyals. Despite his aura of entitlement, the petulant young man was defeated. Much like the ancient camel market, it wasn't about how carefully your *ghuttra* was folded. Do you have the cash? He was all *ghuttra* and no camels.

Before Abu Ali closed the bid, the young man turned and walked off with his entourage, trying to give the impression that he didn't care anyway. Abu Ali said, "Sold," and the whole gallery went up in applause for Yayha. He acknowledged his fans like a bantam-weight boxer who just won on a KO and handed Musa a paper bag full of hundred-riyal bills. Musa didn't even look in the bag as he slid out of the Imperial, and Yayha hopped in. Musa bent over to power the front seat forward and show him a few of the controls before the grinning Yemeni drove off triumphantly in the baby-blue Lebaron.

Wandering around the field, I saw plenty of cars and trucks but not the object of my affection. So I walked along the perimeter lined by haphazard rows of vehicles three deep. I turned at the corner to walk down the far side of the yard and twenty yards in front of me spotted a Saudi National Guard Volvo Laplander for sale. It was love at first sight as I hurried forward. But then, being highly sophisticated about

Suqcraft, I slowed down and totally ignored the Volvo as I ambled past it to a battered Dodge pickup truck with a hard 150,000 miles on the odometer and more on its alignment. As I pretended to examine the truck, a pudgy, middle-aged Saudi with a two-day beard on a large jaw and a white *guffiyeh* atop his closely shaved head, came up to introduce himself. "My name is Hamud," he said in Arabic.

"Glad to meet you. My name is Tim."

"Tim? I don't know this name."

"Oh, in Arabic there is no Tim. In Arabic my name is Khamis." Because I was born on a Thursday, Yom al-Khamis.

"Khamis. Yes, I know that name." He replied. "Are you American?"

"Yes I'm American, but I was born in Dhahran."

"Aramco? My nephew works for Aramco in Ras Tanura. He's a mechanic."

"Now, I work at the King Faisal Specialist Hospital. I make videos to teach Saudi medical students."

"Are you a doctor?"

"Oh no, I make films and videos. I'm trying to help grow Saudi doctors."

Hamud blinked twice, and his jet black eyes became very still. His big jaw shifted a bit and relaxed. "This is very good. The truck, she is 15,000 riyals."

"Fifteen thousand riyals! She is *ajuusah*, an old woman, who doesn't have 5,000 miles left in her."

"Not this truck, that one," and he swept his arm to the Volvo behind me. He must have pegged me on sight. He gave me the full rundown on the jeep. The ubiquitous Yemeni kid jumped in and fired up the engine, and it idled contently, as Hamud showed me the many features of this highly customized Saudi National Guard Volvo Laplander.

The floor was made of quarter-inch Swedish steel diamond plate to protect against land mines as well as lower the truck's center of gravity and make it less likely to roll over. The drive shaft from the engine to the back axle was protected by a steel skid strip. The Volvo's giant tires gave it about two feet of clearance between the ground and the skid plate.

I hopped into the driver's seat, and Hamud sat in the passenger seat to explain the stick transmission - and what a miracle transmission it was. Four gears in 2-wheel drive, four gears in 4-wheel drive that was engaged with a convenient lever in the cab, and then another four gears in Ultra Low 4-wheel drive mode. Basically in Ultra Low-Low the Volvo could climb out of a steep ravine like a mountain goat or tow a fire hydrant horizontally.

I later learned from Rory, the manager of the Volvo dealer's garage, that the gearbox alone cost $15,000 (about $40,000 in 2014 adjusted dollars.) I first met the wiry Irishman from Belfast when I went to get a replacement water pump. Rory was overwhelmed trying to manage a decrepit eight-car garage for a dealership selling twice that many a day. As usual, the parts counter was a mob scene, but when he saw me, he lit up. Finally a mid-twenties Westerner like himself has walked into this mélange of Arabs, Asians, and Africans shouting in half a dozen languages. He waves me into his office, and he closes the door and says with a toothy grin, "My name is Rory. What's yours?"

We hit it off and start talking about the expatriate life in town, what we do and various rumors. He orders two Pepsis, and we are generally living it up as plays his latest Peter Gabriel cassette. Then he tells me a very funny story about the time as teenagers, he and his equally car-crazed cousin Ned scraped together enough money for the boat fare to France. They hitchhiked to Le Mans for the Grand Prix. Living on coffee, cigarettes, and sweet rolls, they arrived in the late afternoon of the start. But instead of finding a good spot to watch the race in town, they sneaked into the woods that bound one of the remote parts of the track. When darkness fell, they inched up to the shoulder of the road, as close to the track as they dared go, and laid down on the gravel.

Prone on the shoulder, they hear a racecar approaching, louder and louder, until it roars past at more than 200 miles per hour, and its wake lifts their bodies a foot in the air and drops them. The cars come in packs. Rory and Ned are being bounced off the ground by racecars speeding three feet away from their heads. "I tell you, Tim, it was like I was freaking flying." They did this late into the night. It was one of those vivid scenes that depict the best part of being young — and foolish, too.

Hamud finished his pitch, and I was about to take the jeep for a spin when the call to evening prayer sounded, and the din of the arena began to settle. I pulled out a thousand riyals as a deposit and said I'd return tomorrow with a friend to check out the mechanicals and close the deal. He pushed the money away and shook my hand, "I'll see you tomorrow, Mr. Khamis."

Photo by David Hills 1975

DRIVING RIYADH: KING OF THE WADI

I returned the next afternoon with Phil, a friend of mine who was a biomedical engineer at the hospital and an enthusiastic car guy from Tennessee. When we arrived, the car *suq* was in its full chaotic splendor. We waded into the swirling confusion for a half-paces until Phil froze and slowly swiveled his head a full 180 degrees, absolutely amazed by this tableau of grinding gears, shouting auctioneers, clouds of burnt rubber and diesel exhaust, popped clutches, and screeching brakes.

After I introduced Hamud to Phil, he inspected the Volvo's suspension and brakes, checked the engine's oil and water, and we test-drove the Volvo around the city streets with the Yemeni kid as navigator. It seemed good to me, and Phil agreed, so we drove back to the *suq*. For some reason, Phil had to leave, and before I could start the price negotiations, Hamud led me off to one of the nearby coffee houses thatched with palm fronds. There were about 30 men talking, drinking tea, smoking the narghile, who studiously ignored us — though they saw everything. We sat at a rickety table on equally rickety painted, wooden chairs joined by woven jute, drank sweet tea, and talked about everything except the price of the Volvo.

The price was a bit of a problem because I only had 13,000 riyals to spend. In a month I would have much more, but in Riyadh, whether you're selling camels or cars, it's strictly cash. My only hope of closing this deal was to employ my primitive bargaining techniques learned buying firecrackers in Khobar. I was more forlorn because I knew that even at 15,000 riyals the Laplander was an absolute steal.

Hamud was from Anaizah, a city several hundred miles north of Riyadh. *If you were born in Dhahran, are you a Saudi? No, I'm a son of Aramco. How is it that you speak Arabic (as pathetically mangled as it is)?* He had three sons, and I had a daughter.

He wanted to know about the hospital. Was it only for royalty and rich people? No, it's a specialist hospital. It's not for the richest, but the sickest. They will be sent from all over the kingdom. Is it open now? No, it's still being built, maybe in six months it will open. Doctors and nurses and technicians are just now arriving to make it ready. Six months? Yes, six months. He nodded to himself and said, "Why aren't you a doctor?"

I laughed, "I'm not smart enough to be a doctor. I make cinema of famous doctors performing operations to be shown to Saudi medical students. Sometimes, I shoot films that demonstrate to nurses how to care for a patient, how to move him carefully. And sometimes I make videos to explain to the janitors about germs and how to use the cleansers and machines to eliminate them. You need all these things in a hospital."

Hamud nodded and offered to get us a hubbly-bubbly, but I declined. At the time I didn't realize that I was sort of a trophy American in that coffee house, nor did I realize that I was probably the only American Hamud had ever talked with. I wasn't sure how I was going to bring up the price of the Laplander, but I didn't have to.

He looked me in the eye and rocked his jaw into not quite a smile, but a benign tilt, "The Swedish is 12,000 riyals."

"12,000 riyals!"

"Yes, 12,000 riyals."

"But I thought you said…"

"Yes, 12,000 riyals."

I wanted to hug him. My hand shot out, "Mr. Hamud, it's a deal."

"Yes, Mr. Khamis, it's done, *khalaas.*" He shook my hand, put his other hand over mine and broke that wide jaw into a grin.

I paid him; he made out a bill of sale and handed me the keys. Hamud told me to return to this coffee house in three days at eight o'clock with 900 riyals to pay for the plates and registration papers — tax and license, as they say in America.

I asked him, "Who should I ask for?" He thought that was really funny.

"Mr. Khamis, you take a seat, and I'm sure the agent will find you." I said good night to Hamud and drove off into Riyadh as the twilight faded into night.

Riyal for riyal, the Volvo jeep was an incredible price for the perfect desert vehicle. Built on the design of a workhorse Swedish farm vehicle, it was armored and powered by a golden gear box. It was too good to be true. I had seen plenty of Saudi National Guard Volvos driving around town with soldiers in the back, so of course the obvious question was how did my jeep end up in the open market?

Perhaps it was surplused because it required more maintenance than it was worth. Except my jeep's tires were much better than theirs, and it had fewer miles too. Most likely this jeep had fallen through various friendly bureaucratic cracks into the private sector. It was more than a little suspicious that I was picking up the plates in a coffee house, but it wasn't for me to judge. I just wanted some sort of quasi-legal ownership.

In the evening, three days later, I pulled up in my new rig, parked on the street and headed into the *suq*. It was subdued, the field was empty and the molehills deserted, but the cafes were busy. I checked out Hamud's lot, but he wasn't around, so I went to the coffee house, found a table against the thatched wall, ordered tea and pretended to blend in, without any hope of that ever happening.

Eventually, I did hang around long enough that I became less of a novelty, and the customers went back to their business. It was a low-ceilinged, dark room punctuated with bare, low-watt bulbs dangling here and there. The plaintive voice of Mohammed Abdu on the radio floated over a dozen conversations from clusters of men drinking tea and smoking cigarettes, bantering back and forth in a low rumble. There was an open kitchen at the back manned by a couple of Yemeni cooks and ten-year-old waiters conveying tea and morsels to the house and out into the night.

With my back to the wall, I was vacantly watching all of this unfold when Adnan dropped into the chair across from me. A plump thirty-something with a terrific barber — his thick hair swept back, his mustache and goatee manicured to precision — and a great tailor. His high *thobe* collar was precisely stitched to fit. He placed a large manila envelope on the table.

"Mr. Khamis."

"Yes."

"I am Adnan."

"Glad to meet you, Mr. Adnan. Would you like some tea?"

"Thank you, but I can only stay a minute."

I put the envelope with 900 riyals on the table. He pushed his envelope to me.

"Look inside. Two plates and the registration book."

I peeked at the plates and removed the flimsy, cardboard registration book. It had a stamp or two, the description of the jeep and some indecipherable signatures. Adnan plucked the book from my hands and said, "This is license. Mr. Khamis. You must, *lazeem*, always have this with you." And gave me a deep, eye-piercing stare for emphasis.

So pleased to take ownership, I was sort of giddy, I grinned at Adnan and replied, "*Lazeem,* I understand. Thank you."

Adnan shook my hand and departed. Who knows how many more license plates he had to deliver that night?

I've lived in Dhahran, Jeddah, and Riyadh, and if you really love to drive in the desert, Riyadh is your only choice. Within an hour, you can visit stony plains as far as the eye can see, traverse pristine, golden sand dunes, tour the craggy cliffs of the Tuwaiq Escarpment or the quiet canyons of Wadi Hanifa, the pools of Al Kharj or head north to Buraidah. You can drive for hundreds of miles in any direction without a fence or obstruction of any kind. At any time you can stop, turn off your engine, and step out into a silence that has always been there.

Some weeknights, my wife Janet, daughter Khamisah, and I would drive the Laplander into the empty desert a few miles north, on the rising ground above the hospital, and have a picnic watching the city below us. Nowadays, we would have been parked in the middle of some dense neighborhood that extended for miles all around.

Then, it was nothing but rocky desert, calm and peaceful. Framed by a tar-black sky riddled with stars. On the weekends, my friends and I would caravan to a specific place or just drive in some arbitrary direction. No matter what we found, every trip was a great trip. I won't go on about our various adventures except for two.

Some miles southeast of Riyadh, I was driving along with my friend Ben Michaels riding shotgun over a faint dirt track through a rolling desert covered with clumps of bushes and gentle drifts feathered with dead grasses. We intersected a well-worn trail, so I turned left and carried on. We weren't exactly lost, but we were a little sketchy about our exact location.

At the time, I was growing a beard and wearing a khaki work shirt with a *ghuttra* around my neck. Ben's *ghuttra* was around his brow like a sweat band. The road dipped, and when we came up to the rise… there was a Saudi National Guard encampment a hundred yards in front of us.

I slowed down. There was a long, steel-pipe gate counterbalanced with a drum of concrete and three armed soldiers who were now staring at me. This really wasn't the time to pull a U-ee and streak away, so I sped up just a bit. About 20 yards away the barrier started to lift; by the time I was at the entrance, the gate was up, and the soldiers saluted me as I drove into the camp. I wasn't about to push my luck, so I nodded to a few curious watchers, quickly turned around the Volvo, and saluted the soldiers as I drove away on important Saudi National Guard business.

Photo by David Hills 1976

Sometime later, somewhere south of the Wadi Hanifa, I was driving the Laplander with Ben in his Toyota Land Cruiser, when we saw a range of very small dunes maybe only six or eight feet tall. It seemed that if we crossed these dunes we'd be at the mouth of the wadi and be able to drive north. I put the Swedish into 4-wheel drive, low-low, and tapped on the gas. With no effort at all the jeep crawled up slip faces and down into the lows before another steep climb. Up and down I drove, over a dozen dunes when I began to believe that I was boldly going forth over terrain never before touched by humanity. A true desert explorer.

I crested the ridge of yet another dune and nearly ran over a single, gnarled flip-flop burnt into an amber crust by the sun. So much for that delusion of grandeur. I pressed on, over the dunes that started getting smaller and then dissolved into the wide mouth of a wadi paved with cobble-stone rocks leading up into a canyon.

We stopped to consider the next step in an entirely vague plan from the start. With the trucks turned off, in the quiet of a cool wind billowing from the wadi, we decided to drive over the stones and up the ravine until we could find a shoulder above the stream bed that we could follow back to town.

I took the lead, and the rocks soon turned into smooth, misshapen volleyball-sized stones and then boulders and bigger boulders. It was great fun navigating through this stone maze, up and around granite rocks the size of bales of hay. I had just maneuvered between two boulders and over a third one when it occurred to me that for sure no one had ever been here before. I was passing over untainted ground.

Only my off-road driving savvy and a superb desert vehicle had now made it possible for me to be the King of the Wadi. And I began to like the sound of that as it echoed in my head.

There was a bend in the canyon; I rolled 20 yards forward and turned up the dry gulch. To the right was a steep slope that fell directly to the dry riverbed, to the left there was a shelf, a shoulder above a yard-high bank. I drove a little farther forward until I could see all the way around the bend – and there it was.

The pride and joy of 1970s Detroit parked beneath an acacia tree on the river bank. Four thousand pounds of American steel packaged in a sleek, slab-like, sheet metal body, trimmed in chrome, with white walled tires and power steering. It was an emerald green, four-door Buick sedan with the trunk open.

Surrounded by several small children, a husky man with thick black hair and a prominent mustache was tending a coffee pot next to a small fire. A woman, probably his wife, ducked behind the sedan. He slowly stood up. He was wearing a *wazzara*, something like a half sarong, around his waist and an undershirt. He seemed to be very happy and cheerfully smiled at me as I drove by. The kids hopped around and waved; his wife peeked from behind the Buick.

Humbled once again, I ruefully waved back and rumbled up the canyon thinking about this man who had adroitly maneuvered that heavy, soft-springed, low-riding, two-wheel drive behemoth all the way down this perilous wadi without even scratching his white walls. No wonder that he was practically laughing at me. I started laughing too. I had just met the real King of the Wadi: an enthusiastic Saudi dad determined to throw a terrific picnic for his family in a magical desert canyon.

POSTSCRIPT

At King Faisal Hospital I worked with two of my closest childhood friends from Dhahran, Mike Benjamin and David Hills. We had a fine time driving around in the desert together, and each of us had a son in the same year. We posed with them in front of our trucks.

Left to right: Mike and Jeff, Tim and Luke, David and Liston – Riyadh 1976

Half Moon Bay - 1954 - *Courtesy of Laurie Wright*

SKI HALF MOON!

By the early 50s, the extravagant waterskiing shows at places like Cypress Gardens in Florida had ignited a rage for waterskiing that swept the nation. A sport that combined blue water, fast boats, beautiful women, and daring young men performing death-defying tricks under the summer sun was the perfect expression of America's post-war exuberance.

At the same time in Arabia, there were a lot of mid-20 or 30-something bachelors working for Aramco as drillers, managers, welders, pilots, engineers, dentists, and master machinists who made Half Moon Bay a waterskiing paradise. Sadly there was a limited number of bachelorettes to impress with their prowess, but if that didn't work out, they still had a helluva great time speeding over the warm, clear water and eventually falling, pinwheeling across the surface to their doom.

It was a great deal of fun. The water-skiers got together for beach picnics and parties, so it was natural that during a wild New Year's Eve bash they hatched a plan for something truly special.

It boggled the imagination, a construct beyond the wildest fever dream of any Sufi mystic, a structure never seen before in the long history of the Arabian Gulf. They built a ski jump.

Basically a plywood ramp built on an 8-by-16-foot raft floating on oil drums — much like a skateboard configuration that you'd see today. The front lip of the jump started below the waterline and ended with you 8-plus feet in the air trying to land without breaking something.

Half Moon Bay - 1954 - *Courtesy of Laurie Wright*

I can pretty much guess how this beast got built in the shops: off the record. And I truly understand that Aramco's transportation department somehow misplaced the work order that sent a giant flatbed Kenworth truck and a forklift to deliver a large, unspecified object to Half Moon Bay. However, I don't have the slightest clue as to how it was officially allowed in the water, anchored 50 feet offshore and about 200 yards east of the crumbling Coast Guard station at the head of the bay – almost halfway to the Yacht Club on the point.

I presume that there was a cordial outreach by the water-skiers to the three or four totally neglected Coast Guard men living in the shabby building without even a boat of their own. A few cases of Pepsi and frequent hundred-pound bags of ice were much appreciated, so the sailors could not have cared less what these Americans did. They were there for smugglers, not water-skiers.

That summer is the golden age of ski-jumping in Saudi Arabia. One day Milt and I drift down from the clubhouse a few hundred yards and watch maniac skiers hit the ramp and go flying into thin air – for better or worse. Everyone makes it off the ramp, but landings are problematic.

Ski-jumping is a bit flawed as a spectator sport because you have to wait for the boat to make a long loop back to the jump, if it comes at all. As the skiers thin out, we begin to lose interest and start heading back to the club when we hear a screaming whine headed our way. It's a sleek Italian-looking runabout driven by a vainly handsome, bare-chested young man wearing a wide grin and mirrored aviator shades. Behind the boat is a long towline, so for a second we can't see what's happening.

It's a long, thin line with someone at the end. The boat comes closer, and we realize that there is a small woman at the end of the ski rope. At the last moment the speedboat swerves and launches her onto the ramp. We finally realize who she is and watch our petite, glamorous art teacher Miss Parker fly at least a dozen feet into the air and pin a perfect landing before she disappears across the water.

By October it was too cold to ski, and the jump was neglected. Winter storms snapped a couple of the raft's anchor lines, some of the oil drums rusted through and flooded. By the next summer, the ski jump was a drifting, lopsided, broken relic covered with barnacles. Occasionally some mad man would attempt to jump it, but he'd be lucky not to fall and be shredded alive.

However, none of this mattered because, after months of agonizing about the cost of a boat versus the perpetual expenses of a family of six children, my dad, Tom, chose the boat.

A mid-level manager at the time, comfortable enough, he drove a 1950 Humber pickup truck, had to watch his cash flow, and the boat was a reach. This decision was followed by a long, involved process to figure out what kind of boat. After lengthy discussions with his circle of experts and pals, my dad decided.

It was late May when the shipment arrived. A fourteen-foot Grumman aluminum boat, a custom trailer to haul it, and a sturdy Evinrude outboard motor, maybe 50 horsepower, I don't really know. My dad was always irked that the trailer cost nearly a third of the boat.

The Grumman opened a whole new aquatic world to us. We were at Half Moon Bay every weekend. Trolling the coast for skipjack, lingering over fishing holes at the third reef. You could plainly see a 20-pound *hamoor* in the clear water ten feet below and easily work your lure to within a foot of his gulping jaws. But these groupers hadn't survived for eons by being stupid. Most of the time they'd slowly move on. Somewhere embedded in the darkest recesses of a *hamoor's* tiny brain there is a line of code that says, "If it's too good to be true, swim away." And they did, except for the one or two guys that didn't get the memo.

One weekend, my dad, my brother, Mike, and I took the boat about halfway to Salt Mine Point. Nowadays it's called Qarriyah, where a sprawling, industrial complex of desalination plants pumps millions of gallons of water to Riyadh every day.

Tom steered the Grumman right up to the shore and beached it in two feet of water. There was not a person within miles, and for as far as you could see in either direction, the long straight beach was exactly as it was a thousand years ago — deserted. We hauled our supplies up to the high tide line, built a fire, cooked our hot dogs, and watched the stars until we drifted off in our sleeping bags to the sound of very small waves lapping softly on the shore.

My dad loved waterskiing. He was really good at it and, though he was in his mid-forties and wouldn't have risked the ski jump in its heyday, he became quite agile on one slalom ski, slashing back and forth across the wake as my godfather Steve Furman sped us across the bay. Eight years old and the size of a tall rhesus monkey, I was the spotter.

A bright-eyed, lanky 14-year-old, my sister Annie was a natural athlete and terrific horsewoman with plenty of *gymkhana* blue ribbons to her name. She was eager to waterski and mastered it almost immediately.

To a passing Bedouin the sight of our speeding boat trailing a very long rope held by a ninety-pound girl who waves as she passes would make no sense at all and definitely provide much food for thought.

But Annie is having a great time. Tom is chilling at the wheel. The motor is purring, the Grumman is slicing through the water, and Half Moon Bay salt spray mists the air. All is good. And then it isn't.

I had just turned to look to the bow, and we both saw it at the same time. There was really nothing we could do. It was less than fifty yards ahead of us, and there was nowhere to turn. Tom couldn't stop or even veer off because Annie might lose her grip. And fall into a giant swirling pod of jellyfish.

He has to steer straight through it, and Annie just has to hold on or else.

Near the end of summer, the jellyfish bloom. A very pale, almost translucent blue, they are about the size of half a soccer ball with a feathery fringe and a bunch of stubby tentacles covered with hundreds of spring-loaded stingers that fire on contact.

They aren't too bad to swim around because there are usually just one or two, here and there. However under certain tidal and current conditions they would be swept together into a swirling pod. A 150-foot circle packed tight with thousands of jellyfish caught in a strange and deadly Sargasso Sea.

I spin to watch Annie. She hasn't seen the jellies yet, but then the water turns pale with their multitude. She realizes what's happening. My heart is in my throat. My sister will certainly die if she falls.

White knuckling the tow-rope handle, Annie shifts into some other gear that she didn't even know existed, sets her jaw, and breaks into a crooked grin as if this dangerous challenge were going to be more fun than ever.

Her skis are slapping over jellyfish as if they are cobblestones made of small, squishy pillow cases. I quiver every time she cuts over another one. My dad is freaked out trying to get through this mess as fast as possible – but not too fast or she might tumble. I'm watching Annie trying to decide. If she falls, will I jump into all those tentacles to save her?

And the pod never ends, I can't even see the water, all I can see is Annie skiing over a living surface of pulsating, pale blue-white jellyfish. Her knees are shaking, her arms are trembling, and her grin is now a straight line of grim determination.

Tom yells, "Here we go! Here we go!"

We're almost out of the pod. Annie skis through the last twenty feet of jellyfish and into the clear water of the bay. She skis about another hundred yards before she falls — in the right place. Annie's beaming when we pick her up. In the boat, my dad lifts her like a feather and hugs her closely. He's so relieved and so proud of Annie. I'm still dumbfounded that she has defied an unimaginable death by poisonous tentacles.

Annie takes off her bathing cap, shakes her hair out. She's young, lithe, and beautiful, hopping up and down, triumphant and manic with glee. We're all happy as my dad trolls along the coast a bit and then heads home. She doesn't ask to ski back to the Yacht Club.

Emir bin Jiuwi's Palace in Hofuf – *John Lunde 1954*

THE AC MEN

This is a dramatized narrative based on actual events and characters. The last line is a verbatim quote from my dad Tom Barger who was there.

Until 1953 it was legal for Americans to drink alcohol within their compounds. His Majesty King Abdul Aziz ibn Saud granted this privilege to the oilmen in appreciation of their heroic efforts to extinguish the runaway oil fire at Dammam #12 in June of 1939.

So Aramco operated a liquor store based on a monthly ration coupon basis and served beer in the Stag Club where the oilmen gathered to relax, play cards, and shoot billiards or the breeze. It was a men's club, not by choice; for most of its history, there were fewer than a dozen single women in the whole town.

So it's 1952 on a late Thursday afternoon, and two of the foremen in charge of building the air-conditioning network throughout the entire camp are playing cribbage in the club, enjoying their day off. I'll call them Don and Paul. Don is a stout, brash plumber who is sensitive about the bulging spare tire saddled around his waist. Paul is a tall, slouching electrician with a hangdog expression like Walter Matthau. They're both from New Jersey, having a few cans of Iron City beer — the only brand that Aramco served — talking about baseball, minding their own business, when Burt Simmons, the crusty, old timer camp foreman appears at their table.

"Do you want the bad news first?"

"What's the good news?" asks Paul.

"Well, from what I could patch together I think the AC unit has probably blown a fuse. It should be easy to fix."

Don says, "The bad news…"

Apologetically Burt says, "It's in Dammam."

"Dammam!" they blurt out together.

"Yes, Dammam. At bin Jiluwi's palace. Quint says to get it done."

The son of Abdullah, one of the most famous warriors in Saudi history, Emir Saud bin Jiluwi is the governor of al

Hasa, the Eastern Province of Saudi Arabia. He holds absolute dominion over the desert east of Riyadh, from Kuwait in the north to the boundless dunes of the Rub' al-Khali.

Quint is a grasping, always-well-dressed assistant to the district manager, and his boss is on short leave in Beirut. As the acting district manager, there isn't a thing in this world that Quint won't do for Emir Saud bin Jiluwi.

Quint calls Burt, "Bin Jiluwi's palace has gone down. There is no air conditioning. Get someone to fix it."

"Wait a minute. What are you talking about? Why should I care?"

"Because. Because it's bin Jiluwi."

"Do you have a number that I can call back and figure out what's exactly wrong?"

"Never mind. He said that the motor stopped. It's probably a blown fuse. Get going. I promised him that we'd have some guys there in an hour."

"Who said?"

"His name is Selim. He's the emir's top guy. Ask at the palace when you get there."

"Me?"

"No, them. Find some guys. Gotta go."

Burt buys another round of Iron City, convinces Don and Paul that it will be a snap, and offers to authorize eight hours of triple overtime. This plan probably isn't Burt's best idea, but then he is low on options and has other things to do.

Paul hops into Don's completely fitted-out Dodge Power Wagon, and they depart the Stag Club on the way north about 20 miles to Dammam. In 1952 there is nothing between Dhahran and Dammam except a few rocky ridges, a lot of flat desert, and a lonely, two-lane asphalt road, barely populated by cabs, pickup trucks, jitney buses, and Kenworths. The Dodge doesn't have AC, so the windows are down as they drive on.

Twice Don has to stop to let herds of camels cross the blacktop. In town, he is stalled in a narrow street behind a donkey cart heavily laden with sacks of dates. It has a flat tire. Finally they pull up in front of the palace gate. There is an older, stone-faced guard in a khaki uniform holding a rifle with a fixed bayonet. Paul walks up to him and asks for Selim.

He glowers at the electrician and says, "Selim?"

"I don't know. Selim. Selim!" says Paul as he waves his hands in frustration.

The suspicious guard starts to raise his rifle before Paul blurts out, "Selim. AC. Fix AC."

It's a funny thing but almost immediately after the Americans arrived, AC became an Arabic word. The guard relaxes and says, "Selim. Condition?" using the Arabic synonym for AC.

"Yes. Condition. Selim."

The guard is all smiles as he whistles up his youngest, scrawniest recruit to guide the guys, not to the palace, but to a low-lying building next to it. It's the barracks of the palace guard. Before they can get out of the truck, a thin, middle-aged Kenyan with thick, slicked-black black hair wearing a white polyester short-sleeve shirt and a ready grin greets them in a broken English accent.

"Sahib. So good to see you, I knew you'd help."

Don says, "Selim?"

"At your service. Yes, sir, Selim. I'm company clerk for Abu Jumbia,"

"Abu Jumbia?

"Yes, sahib, Abu Jumbia – it means father of the dagger. He's the governor's chief body guard and commander of the company."

Don thought he was driving out to fix the governor's AC, but he is suddenly eager to please the Father of the Dagger.

Paul interjects, "How come you speak such good English?"

"Yes, sahib, I was a hotel clerk in Nairobi for many years. But then I came here."

Don wants to know why of all places Selim came to Dammam, but he doesn't have the heart to ask. Instead, he asks where the AC unit is located. He and Paul quickly figure out the problem. A rodent has chewed into the main power cable and shorted out both himself and the AC. It's easy to repair, and less than an hour later, they are driving back to Dhahran as dusk descends over the desert.

For some reason, almost lost to posterity, Don and Paul start bickering, then arguing with each other. Maybe it was the special bottle of Swedish Solvent in Paul's toolbox that was talking. The two men start screaming at each other, louder and louder. Bubbling with anger, Don steers off the road, across the gravel shoulder, and screeches to a halt ten yards away in the hard-packed desert sand.

The truck is still running as both men burst out of the cab and attack each other before they even clear the hood. They grapple and fall to the sand. Paul gets stabbed in the side by a sturdy, desiccated twig half-buried in the sand. His distress allows Don to stand up and call him out. Paul staggers to his feet and says, "Give me your best shot, Doughnut Man."

It's on. They exchange wide, slow punches, charge, and curse at each other in front of the Power Wagon's headlights, which act as a stage-right, directional spotlight on a desert stage amidst the blackness of night. From the road, Don and Paul appear as silhouetted stick figures engaged in a stroboscopic, slow-motion Punch and Judy act.

This is a strange story based on actual events, but it becomes even stranger when a Saudi I'll call Adnan comes driving by in his uncle's '49 Chrysler on an errand to Dhahran. Most every large family has an Adnan. Unmarried, late-twenties, he wants so many things but hasn't the ambition to earn them. Plus, even his cousins find him a bit unreliable.

Inexplicably, Adnan screeches to a halt and launches himself into the fight. Nobody will ever know why he did this, but from the road now it looks like three stick figures grappling like Kabuki wrestlers in the desert.

Unfortunately for everyone involved, Corporal Aziz has checked out early from his post at the Dhahran police station and hitched a ride to Qatif with a dump truck filled with scrap metal bought surplus from Aramco. He is dreaming of a quiet Friday with his wife and kids when he arrives at the scene. As if you could miss it. Three guys panting and stumbling in the headlights of the idling Dodge truck.

Still in his uniform, Aziz wades into the exhausted scrum of three men, separates, and talks to each one of them. Neither Don nor Paul nor Aziz understand a word spoken between themselves. Adnan is aggrieved. He tells Aziz that the two Americans robbed him of 200 riyals.

The beauty of a dump truck is that it can always accommodate three prisoners in its bed and quite elegantly deposit them in front of the Dammam jail if necessary.

Friday morning, my dad, Tom Barger, who works in Aramco's government relations, drives to the Dammam jail. He brings the guys bottled water and rations of sardines, oranges, cheese, and bread. Don and Paul, beat-up and hungover as they are, won't say what the fight was about. But neither of them had the slightest idea as to how Adnan appeared. All of a sudden he was brawling with them. They certainly didn't rob him of 200 riyals.

Two days later, with his witty, well-traveled translator Suliman, Tom drives back to the courthouse in Dammam. It's a wide room with a tall plaster ceiling and two languid fans barely rotating from above. The perimeter is lined with sturdy, upholstered bolsters to accommodate a crowd that isn't there today. In the middle of the room are a dozen-plus folding chairs in front of a battered teak desk that was probably new when Lawrence led the raid on Aqaba.

Behind the desk is the *qadhi* or judge; I'll call him Sheikh Hassan. Close to 70 years old, he's a small man with narrow shoulders, a long head, close-cropped gray hair, and four-day stubble. He's wearing a white knit *qaffieyh*, skull cap, and a high-collared, white *thobe* with a Mont Blanc pen in his front pocket. As the courtroom settles, his light gray eyes sweep the room like a magnet picking up iron fillings.

Sheikh Hassan states that there are two charges against Don and Paul: public disturbance and robbery for 200 riyals. Through Suliman, my dad, acting as a sort of defense attorney, explains that the fight was purely a matter of honor. Only between them, at night, in the middle of the desert halfway to Dhahran – as far away from the public as possible. As to the second count, they each made almost 200 riyals a day, so why would they rob Adnan?

Shaikh Hassan listens impassively, only his silver hawk eyes scanning my dad and Suliman, as they talk back and forth to make their case. Next, the plaintiff is called to testify.

Lean and handsome, wearing an immaculate, brilliant white *thobe*, ironed to perfection by his maiden aunt, and his red-and-white-checked *ghuttra* — folded just right — Adnan states his case. After a few questions from the *qadhi*, he launches into a diatribe about Don and Paul that Suliman can barely translate fast enough. He rattles on until Hassan cuts him off with a nod of his chin.

Adnan's story is that he was driving along, saw two Americans fighting each other, thought it was his civic duty to break up the brawl, intervened, and they robbed him of 200 riyals. Hassan asks him a few more questions and then calls on the first defendant.

Suliman beckons to Don who approaches the judge. The sheikh asks if he will testify under oath. "Oath?" thinks Don. He really wants to get out of the Dammam jail. So sure, "I'll swear an oath."

The judge stares at Don for a long moment, rolls his chair back, reaches into his worn, wooden desk and brings out a thick, faded blue cotton bag. He lays it on the desktop, pulls out a large black book and motions to his bailiff who picks it up and delivers it to Don. My dad can't believe what he is seeing. It's a Bible.

Qadhi Hassan asks for the plumber's oath on the *Book of the Christians*. With his hand on the Bible, Don pledges that he will only tell the truth. The bailiff retrieves the good book and Hassan quizzes Don about the circumstances that night.

As he relates the events of that evening in a soft, hoarse voice, Don is downcast, haggard, and weary. The shiner on his left eye is starting to mend — it looks much better than it did Thursday night. Whether it's in Arabic or English, his body language speaks for a humbled, contrite man — who will certainly never do that again.

At the end of his testimony, Don states that neither he nor Paul in any way robbed Adnan. Sheikh Hassan silently considers his statement and then asks, "After this fight, is Paul still your friend?"

"Oh, yes," says Don, "He's my best friend here in Arabia. We just had an argument about the Yankees and Dodgers."

Suliman, the wiley and wordly translator, stumbles and falls at that last remark. Tom interjects in Arabic, "My honor. It's called baseball, a game sort of like cricket for Americans. Professional players can make more than 50,000 riyals a year. The Yankees and the Dodgers are two famous teams who are angry with each other and bitter rivals."

And apparently their fans are hotheads, too, Hassan thinks as he stares back at my dad. His youngest grandson Saif plays for a neighborhood soccer team in Dammam. He's a bit of a soccer granddad and has a very low opinion of the team from Saihat.

The sheikh ends the proceedings without calling Paul. The three defendants are lined up in front of him as he announces that the count of public disturbance is dismissed. It was a private dispute until Adnan, who should have been minding his own business, jumped in.

On the second count the Americans are not guilty. He has asked around and discovered that Adnan rarely has more than 50 riyals to his name.

Hassan calmly looks at Adnan and says, "You have brought false charges against these men. Back to your cell for now."

The hapless Adnan is dragged away by two guards. Don and Paul thank the sheikh before quickly retreating with Suliman to the company car. My dad lingers for a moment and approaches Hassan at his desk to thank him for his generosity to the AC men. They talk in Arabic for a few minutes before Tom asks the question he has been dying to ask, but probably shouldn't: "Your honor, I was surprised that you have a bible. Where did that come from?"

For the first time all day, the judge breaks character. Hassan's face relaxes, a soft grin is almost a smile, those light gray eyes have a new liveliness. Looking up from his desk, he says, "Mr. Barger, you must know that we have been doing this for a very long time. We are all people of the Book."

Sufaniya Bay 2016 - *Google Earth*

WONDER REEF

It was the summer of 1964. Smith and I were 17, working as apprentice divers for the freshly established Al Gossaibi Diving Services, the brain child of the legendary Dee McVey. Dee had been the lead diver and manager of undersea operations for all of Bechtel's offshore projects since the mid-fifties. When Bechtel finished up, Dee recognized a great business opportunity and set up the first Saudi commercial diving operation in the Gulf with his partner Mohammed Al-Gossaibi.

Dee's first dive ship was the *Dhow London* stationed out of Sufaniya. A big, wooden vessel maybe 70 feet long with a robust diesel engine and a crew of eight sailors from all points of the Arabian Gulf: Oman, Bahrain, and Jubail. Lean as whippets, strong as bulls, these men were genuinely happy to be at sea. They were even happier when Smith or I would go overboard at the end of the day with a spear gun and deliver a fat *hamoor*, a distinctive Gulf grouper, for dinner.

Someday I'll write a full account of our adventures on the *London*, but that day the dhow was at the dock in Sufaniya for an engine repair, so Smith and I had the day off. There wasn't a whole lot to do in the camp, so we gathered our snorkeling gear and spear guns and hired a cab. He drove us about a mile, along a sandy trail that eventually ended and dropped us 50 yards away from the head of a small, pristine bay just southeast of town.

I had spotted it earlier when I hitched a ride to Sufaniya on a company DC-3. The bay was shaped like a big blue, reversed apostrophe with its long tail merging into a wide, sandy inlet that spilled into the more-green-than-blue waters of the Gulf. Flying over, I could see dozens of stingrays hovering at the mouth of the bay, and along the edge closest to the Gulf there was a long, dark shadow 30 feet from the shore that had to be a reef.

As the cab drives off, we wade into the shallows. Smith and I are each about six feet, three inches tall, but he has a bigger frame and easily outweighs me by 30 pounds. He also has terrible eyesight, so that he has to fold up his glasses and position them in his mask in order to see anything at all. Not comfortable but it works for him. We adjust our masks, slip on our fins, and slip into the warm, tepid water. Leading with our arbalettes — a spear gun powered by cords of surgical tubing — we use only our flippers to silently swim like porpoises.

The water is about 20 feet deep and clear as gin — the visibility is at least 100 feet, and rising off the clean white sand right before us is a perfect coral reef. About 20 yards wide and the length of a football field, in places a couple of feet from the surface, this magnificent labyrinth of rock and coral is decorated with elaborate elk-horned corals, punctuated with massive brain corals the size of Volkswagens, and swarming with about every sea creature known to the Arabian Gulf.

We snorkel along, easily diving to the bottom if we want to check out a cluster of big clams, closely examine the sea cucumbers, or just glide along the base of the reef. Smith dives down, has a great shot at a hefty *hamoor* but lowers his spear gun and doesn't take it. Underwater he turns to look back to me, and I understand completely. We don't want to break the spell of this virgin reef by fussing with a 20-pound *hamoor* corpse. Especially so early in the day.

He picks up a broken piece of coral and pokes at a luminescent yellow anemone to watch its tentacles retract.

Something catches my eye to the left: it's a cuttlefish slowly cruising along. Its body is changing colors back and forth like a spaceship from Star Trek.

Following quietly, I'm able to get about three feet from the cuttlefish as it cycles its colors from bright green to an electric blue to a shimmering pink. The colors strobe along the edges of the squid in a deeper hue than the rest of its skin. It's very beautiful. I swim too close, and the cuttlefish blasts me with a cloud of ink the size of a beach ball and jets away. I knew about squid shooting ink from 20,000 Leagues Under the Sea, but to actually see that inky blob is a first in my life, as it would be in anyone's life.

The reef is actually long clusters of coral divided by canyons that fall to the bright sandy bottom littered with living shells, mud suckers, starfish, shrimp, and clumps of sea grass populated by hordes of tiny luminous fish. The canyon walls are covered with teeming marine life of all sorts: from the crannies in the coral moray eels stick out their snouts, a sea snake wiggles into a dark hole, and at the foot of the reef I see a lobster's antenna protruding from a crack in the coral.

A four-foot-wide stingray glides just off the sandy bottom along the reef. Its back is mottled into the vivid design of a perfect Persian carpet rendered in maroon, bright yellow, forest green, and pale blue. I can see the ray's whip-like tail and near its base the actual, arrowhead-shaped stinger that does all the damage. But it will never attack you; just don't violate its first commandment: "Don't tread on me."

I take a breath and propel myself through a canyon. Through dozens of angelfish of all kinds. The small ones are white and yellow with a blue stripe and small carmine dots near their fins. The big ones — a foot and a half tall — are painted in severe black and white stripes like a zebra. Slow and stately, they cruise along like show horses, surrounded by a lively traffic of smaller fishes from purple neon guppies to dozens of beautiful fish I wish I could identify.

When you are snorkeling and then dive under the surface, something happens that most people never consider: you hear sound very well because it travels easily under water. About ten feet below the surface, I am quietly swimming past garish green anemones and over mustard yellow fire coral with thousands of fish darting everywhere, and I hear a symphony. It's music to my ears in the way that an overture, an aria, or a steel guitar can transport someone away from all the cares and distractions of life to the peaceful presence of the present. This is a fairly Zen-like thought for a guy that can't even spell Zen, but it was one of those moments.

I hear dozens of faint, discordant chirps like out-of-tune crickets playing over a bass line of continual grinding. It's a parrotfish eating the coral. As big as a shoebox, it has the chompers for the job and patiently eats away at the coral, which is its role in the system. Gliding along, ten feet underwater, listening to the orchestra, I realize that right now I'm part of that system, and I like it.

Trailing behind a fat parrotfish, I'm distracted by a pufferfish slowly coming the other way. I swim after the puffer a bit, and then poke toward it with my spear gun. The puffer instantly explodes into an obese, spiny volleyball, flicks its tail, and swims off.

I hover over some coral about two feet from the surface, holding on to a clump, breathing through my snorkel, watching straight down through my mask at the action. After a minute or two I focus on the different colors splotched across the reef. Everything is painted with variegated lichen ranging from deep greens to magenta and royal blue, pale yellow and violet; colored sponges sprout like mushrooms from the coral. In the cracks there are hundreds of sea urchins of all sizes, prickly with sharp black needles, surrounded by half-opened bivalves, their purple mantles straining the water for plankton.

The longer I stay there drifting over the coral, the more detail I can see. Tiny fishes the size of a lima bean, weird little sea horses fringed with manes that look like seaweed, wild anemones like Medusa's head sprouting from a stem the size of a silver riyal.

Time sort of dissolves, and I'm there for ten or fifteen minutes before a resplendent lionfish appears. Painted with a camouflage-like pattern in shades of yellow, gold, and orange, it is designed not to blend in, but to loudly dare any fish to attack it. About the size of a pigeon, it sports 21 beautiful, deadly, venomous spines, any one of which could paralyze, if not kill, a human. The lionfish is not afraid of anything. I jab at it with my spear gun and, unlike any other fish on the reef, the angry lion fish turns with its bristling quills and advances on me.

Floating like driftwood above the coral in the warm, still water of the bay, wearing only a white tee shirt and cut-off jeans, mesmerized by the riot of color and movement beyond my mask, I am probably as free as I'll ever be in my life. So integrated into this world that maybe, like an ungainly porpoise, I'm just another mammal passing through.

A flashing movement 20 feet out into the bay catches my eye. About two feet below the surface, a gleaming phalanx of chromium needlefish streams by. Sleek, trout-size darts with long, sharp, needle-like beaks, they are flying fish — when the action gets hot, they blast themselves through the surface and into the air, soaring in a low arc about six feet high and 20 feet long before they splash back into the Gulf.

There is a favorite story about "Big Tom." And he was big, close to 300 pounds on a sturdy, barrel-chested frame, three inches short of six feet. In the early afternoon, he and my dad are coming back from fishing the third reef in Tom's boat. It's been a productive day with many *hamoor*. Standing up as he steers the boat home, Big Tom is already savoring grilled grouper drenched in his special cinnamon, curry, and lemon sauce on a bed of that Spanish rice that his wife Maria does so well. He is perfectly content.

Then a burst of dozens of needlefish explodes out of the water, coming straight at him. My dad ducks, two needlefish land in the boat and flop around, but a third kamikaze dives out of the sky to spear Big Tom's substantial left forearm. The needlefish sticks in his flesh like a live, flapping harpoon. Watching this unfold as they speed along, my dad is amazed. And then totally astounded as Big Tom looks down, maintains speed, rips the fish out of his arm, flips it back in the water and, totally unfazed, continues steering as if he had just smacked a mosquito.

Stealthy like patrolling U-boats, three barracuda follow the needlefish less than a foot from the surface. Silver-blue, they are shaped like a six-inch-wide slat in a picket fence. Not more than a yard long, they are extremely fast and endowed with sharp teeth that would make a piranha consider dentures. As they slowly move by, propelled by the merest flick of a fin, I can see their jaws quickly biting the water as if it were meat. They are no threat to me as I watch them follow the needlefish.

I snorkel over to the west edge of the reef, the side facing the bay, and look down its length. It's as if someone has placed a large, intricate, ceramic structure crawling with life on the sandy bottom of a giant aquarium. The white sand ripples with the shadows of the swells above.

Coming straight at me, a couple of yards off the face of the reef, is a big green sea turtle. Its broad shell is about four feet long, its head about the size of a toaster, its graceful flippers cycling without the slightest effort. I dive and duck behind a coral head, so I won't spook her, and watch this marvelous creature, one of the oldest reptiles on earth, pass by.

Less than ten feet away, I can clearly see her deep, black eyes, her prominent, beak-shaped mouth and gulping jaw. Her smooth shell, shingled around the edge with plates, is a wonder of hydrodynamic engineering. As she paddles away, I'm stunned by the idea that this green turtle is a virtually unchanged descendent of a species that is 100 million years old. When humans were just coming down from the trees, this sea turtle had been swimming the oceans for more than 98 million years.

I'm soon distracted by two sharks gliding toward me. Every skin-diving story needs a couple of sharks to accentuate the drama. Unfortunately, these nurse sharks are less than two feet long, slowly skimming over the bottom.

I'm familiar with these sharks. There were always dozens of them hovering in the shallow waters off the pier in Dammam. A favorite spearfishing spot, the pier was six miles long but less than ten feet deep for the first half-mile. In three feet of water I grabbed my first mud shark.

About a foot and a half long, it twisted and flexed in my hands with surprising strength for such a small creature. It was like gripping the disembodied bicep muscle of some world-class weightlifter. It was an amazing thing to actually feel the sheer strength of a two-foot mud shark, a good reference point for any future encounter with a 12-foot hammerhead.

The two nurse sharks wander down the reef, and in the distance I see a large cloud of silver fish about the size of very large sardines streaming toward me. At the slightest vibration they all split off with perfect synchronization. Darting together, right or left, up or down. They reassemble into a school before, out of nowhere, Smith strikes from a coral canyon right into them. I had forgotten that Smith was even here. As he darts into the school, they divert around him in a perfect silhouette, as if in an animated cartoon when a character runs through a wall and holes it with his outline. Smith spins to watch them leave, sees me, waves, and points to shore.

We've been on the reef for more than three hours, our throats are dry, and we'd really like something to drink. We slide up near the beach into a couple feet of water, take off our masks and flippers, and un-cock our spear guns. Smith says, "Did you shoot anything?"

"No. Saw a perfect skipjack. Would have been easy. You shoot anything?"

"Had a head shot on fat red snapper, but no. I didn't shoot a thing. I didn't even try."

"It's a wonder, isn't it?"

"Yes, it truly is a wonder."

After I completed this story, I checked out Sufaniya Bay on Google Earth and found the wide satellite photo that I used to headline this tale.

I couldn't lead with this closer shot of the bay in non-living color because it is much too sad.

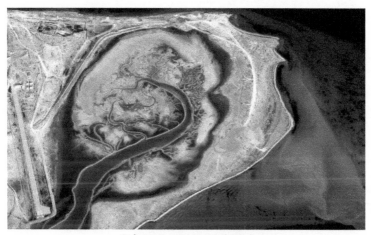

Sufaniya Bay 2016 - *Google Earth*

As you can see, the inlet is now a toxic sump pit, its greasy surface painted by the tides and currents into a strangely beautiful, but deadly plume. The bay is dead; the reef is gone forever. Only the wonder remains.

Old man on the outskirts of Khobar
- *Dorothy Miller 1954*

CENTER OF GRAVITY

Milt and I are hunkered in the oleander bushes along the side yard of my house in Dhahran talking about how to blow up Soviet tanks in Budapest.

In the fall of 1956, the Hungarian freedom fighters had heroically resisted the Russian invaders for two weeks in a totally unequal contest — Molotov cocktails and hunting rifles versus T-54 tanks and heavy artillery. They were brutally crushed just a month ago.

This bloody revolt was our introduction to violent evil and the heroes who fought against it. And this wasn't happening in the past — in Korea, in Okinawa, or on the sandy beaches of Normandy — it was happening now. And we tried to comprehend how this could be.

We eavesdropped on adults discussing the street battles, scrutinized *Time* magazine and the *Herald Tribune*. We listened to BBC on the shortwave radio with our parents, but what pushed us over the edge was a newsreel that played at the theater before some pirate movie that we couldn't wait to see. *The Fall of Budapest* in five minutes of combat footage with a staccato narrator reeling off the bad news. We couldn't wait to fight Russians.

Then we heard the story of a Hungarian teenager whose father was killed by a tank. While its heavy gun traverses the battleground for new targets, the boy picks up a satchel charge, darts through machine gun fire, and dives under the tank to blow it up. He was 13. He wasn't a suicide bomber; he was a Freedom Fighter. We are nine, and we want to be Freedom Fighters, too.

Sitting in the shade, Milt mentions that he found one of those small, glass airline bottles of gin — obviously misplaced, to his dad's deep regret — in the back of a drawer in the garage. We simultaneously know what to do. We'll pour out the gin. Add gasoline and a rag fuse to make our first Molotov cocktail to test in the desert. Sort of a mini-Molotov.

Just then, Doug Strader bangs through the front gate and heads straight to us. "Where've you been? This is cool!

My dad left a bunch of wood at home for us to make boats. Said he'd take us all to Half Moon Bay to float them."

What a terrific idea, but…

"My mom called your moms. It's okay!" With that, we run off down the street to his house. Two years older than us, Doug is a big-boned, blonde-haired kid with an answer for almost any question and a casual regard for the truth. Sad to say, Doug was the first one to tell me about the facts of life, and it has been a confused subject ever since.

When he is with the older kids, Milt and I are basically earwigs, not worth noticing. But when the cool guys leave, he reverts to the Doug I've known my whole life. Crawling together through the elephant grass at Imhoff Gardens, the 20-acre sewage treatment oasis hallway to Al Khobar. Firing off bottle rockets in the desert, throwing jellyfish at each other at the beach, or quietly eating Mars bars under the shade of the eight wooden steps that lead up to the barbershop, watching feet go up and down. We shared 11th Street Dhahran DNA.

There is a long table in his backyard — a piece of plywood on a couple of sawhorses — with scraps of one-inch pine in widths to six inches, saws, hammers, nails, and Will Meadows hard at it building an aircraft carrier. A lanky redhead with a sharp brush cut and a gap between his teeth, Will is one of my best friends and naturally multi-talented — from picking the combination locks on the lockers at school to drawing, freehand, absolutely perfect circles in a row to flipping one-handed cartwheels endlessly across the lawn. He shows us his carrier: a flat piece of light plywood nailed to two 2-by-2-inch runners. He flips it over to show how the superstructure is being built with stacks of 1-by-4s along the flight deck.

Will pulls a plastic bag out of his jeans pocket and says, "Look at this! I got these in Khobar for two riyals a few weeks ago. They'll be perfect." And they are. About a dozen poorly molded replicas of World War One aircraft: biplanes, tri-planes, and four-engine bombers, evidently some kind of set. Each plane is about four inches long, cast in either dark green or dull blue plastic.

Milt and I immediately set to work. After shaping a six-inch-wide board by cutting a picket-fence shape for the bow and sawing it off about a foot and a half back for the stern, we are ready to construct the topsides.

I should mention that although there is no sandpaper to be seen, we wouldn't have known what to do with it anyway. Milt catches a quarter-inch splinter under his left thumbnail. After he stops yelling and thrashing around on the ground, Will grabs his hand, looks closely at the thumbnail, and suddenly bites Milt's thumb. What? Then, to our delight, he spits out the sliver and announces with a bright grin, "I would have grabbed it with my fingers, but I bite my nails."

The arms race resumes. Checking a sketch he has drawn on a paper bag, Doug is methodically building a somewhat realistic version of the battleship *USS Missouri,* Will's aircraft carrier is shaping up, and we are desperately hammering away to build the most improbable battle ships ever designed. They are much taller than they are wide, each layer of pine festooned with small blocks of wood with two-inch nails driven in halfway — these are the cannons. Between us, we sport some 37 cannons. We are ready for action.

And so is Gil Strader. Every day in Dhahran the work whistle blows at five o'clock exactly. About 20 minutes later, Doug's dad ambles out of his back door into the yard, wearing an open khaki work shirt, fishing shorts, and beat-up sneakers.

A barrel-chested man with a slight paunch, he has a large head and the profile of a Roman senator like you'd see in a marble bust at a museum that you were forced to go to with your family. Aside from a kind of benign grin, Gil's facial expression doesn't change that much, but under his slightly hooded eyelids, his pale blue eyes see everything.

We've all known Gil forever and can't wait to show off our fleet. Will has just glued the plastic planes to the deck with Duco cement, so he carefully holds his aircraft carrier level.

"Is that a Fokker Tri-Plane?" says Gil.

"Oh yeah, like the Red Baron flew, and here is a British Sopwith Camel, the plane that shot him down."

"A deadly air force, for sure. Doug, that looks just like the *Missouri*. You have the superstructure just right — good job. What you got there, Milt?"

Milt proudly says, "It's a super battleship. It has 19 guns, Mr. Strader."

"Wow! That's a lot."

"Yeah, one more than Tim's."

"Tim, is that a super battleship, too?"

"Sure is, but it has anti-aircraft guns everywhere," I say, pointing to the dozens of tiny finishing nails I hammered into the deck. It looks like a pin cushion.

"How did it get this mud on it?"

"Camouflage. It'll be harder for the enemy to see."

Gil looks at me for a still second. "Good idea, Tim."

As we go to the car, Gil ducks into his garage and puts a few short pieces of ¾-inch galvanized water pipe and a coil of wire into his tackle box. He stows it in the trunk with his webbed patio chair, the water jug, the ice chest, the bag of wood scraps, and a tarp.

It's around six when we set off for Half Moon Bay in Gil's company car – a red 1955 Ford sedan with official numbers stenciled on the sides. We're all in the back seat chattering away with our ships in hand.

Next to Gil in the front is a basket of sandwiches made by his wife Mitzi and the classic one-quart Thermos bottle - it has a pale green, faux-hammered finish topped with a chrome plated cup and stopper. It must be popular with all Aramco men because on every fishing trip, camping expedition or just driving around in the desert it seems that the green, lightly dented Thermos is always near at hand. It never occurred to me what it might contain besides coffee.

At the Main Gate Gil hangs a left and heads west into the setting sun. After we clear the rocky jebels of Dhahran, there is literally nothing on either side of the road. A few stony ridges in the distance on the left and an almost flat desert as far as I can see from my position next to the right window. It is a completely untouched landscape, and although there is nothing there, it has a magnetic hold on me. The other guys are talking about U-boat warfare, and I'm holding my super battleship, staring out the window.

The sedan slows down to let a flatbed truck turn left on the road to the Yacht Club at Half Moon Bay. We don't turn left. We aren't going to the Yacht Club. Good! We are probably going further around the bay. "Mr. Strader, are we going to Abqaiq beach?"

"Yes, Tim, we are going near there. I found a good place for us."

"Cool."

"Yeah, it's cool."

Watching him drive is very interesting. Eyes forward behind his mirrored aviator shades, his thinning hair fluttering a bit in the wind, his Roman nose, thick lips, heavy jaw, and wide neck — he must have been a tough guy playing football in school. His big hands are like paws lightly touching the wheel. I notice that his complexion is not so smooth; he must have had bad zits when he was a kid. A cool evening breeze is blowing through the car, we are motoring on, and Gil is content.

I didn't know until years later that Gil was a Naval logistics officer for the fleet during D-Day, in charge of the tankers delivering thousands of barrels of gasoline to shore every day. After the war he married Mitzi, worked for Standard of New Jersey, and transferred to Arabia in 1948 to begin a long career as a senior engineer with Aramco.

Mitzi was a very compact force of nature, a trim, vivacious brunette with big, light hazel eyes and a crooked smile. Barely five feet tall, she had the energy of an uncoiled cheetah. Mitzi was entirely confident that the world would be a better place if every kid would just do exactly what she told him to do. Doug, Milt, and I were a continual disappointment. Mitzi was the Den Mother for our Cub Scout pack, and I imagine that she prodded Gil to think of a good project to keep us off the streets. I'm so glad she did.

By 1956 Dhahran had grown from a small oil camp to a slightly larger small town of maybe 3,500-plus Americans, nearly half families, the rest singles. Beyond the camp there was nothing but blank desert until Al-Khobar ten miles away on the coast. Remote and isolated, these Americans created a unique community.

I had never lived anywhere else, so I couldn't really compare Dhahran to any other small town in the States. But I was pretty sure that it was different for a bunch of reasons. What small town gave all of its residents a three-month, paid, transcontinental vacation every two years?

The whole place was like one big neighborhood, and it seemed to me that a lot of the men like my dad and his friends had an almost tribal spirit about passing on their skills and techniques. They taught us kids how to make things, how to dream about ideas to make, and how to consider problems as solutions that you hadn't yet discovered.

Steve Furman and Tom Handzus often took me fishing and attempted to convince me that sardines were edible. Will's dad Gus showed Will and me how to make a rocket sled from the CO_2 cartridge of a seltzer bottle and cheerfully welded together our Kangaroo Bikes. Milt's father was a stand-off dad, but he did snag us a precious carton of small cans of pharmaceutical ether to fuel our model airplane engines.

My neighbor John Ames, a true old-timer in Arabia since 1938, hot-forged a steel trident spearhead before my eyes and then, in the desert ridges just west of Dhahran, taught a 10-year-old boy how to fire an M-1 rifle.

It wasn't until decades later that I realized that he had taken me to the same ridge that in 1941, after Rommel's victories in North Africa, a hundred American oilmen had planned to defend against Nazi paratroopers trying to seize the Dammam field. Their plan was to hold out long enough for the drillers to blow the wells and then all flee south to Qatar. American civilians willing to risk their lives against German soldiers to deny them an oil field in Saudi Arabia. It was truly a world war.

Mr. Ames couldn't have known at the time, but if I had never been on the crest of that ridge, watching him squeeze round after round into targets below, I never would have realized today the price these men were willing to pay.

Gil turns off at the road to Abqaiq beach. We are twitching with anticipation, all talking at once about our naval firepower. A few hundred yards from the bay we bounce in unison as he veers over a sandy berm and fishtails the Ford onto a bumpy trail. He circles a dune to the left and drives up to an isolated, untouched hundred-foot beach bookended by dunes. As we approach the shore, Gil pulls a U-turn and backs the bulbous sedan to the high-tide line.

We burst out of the car and run to the beach. Will slips his aircraft carrier into the water, and it glides forward, slightly lopsided. Doug launches the *Missouri* with a rebel yell, and it capsizes. What?

Milt comes splashing in and shoots his battleship onto the water. It turns over and slides to a stop. I see what is happening and carefully place my super battleship in the water to watch it fall over on its side.

We're standing in the water dumbstruck. "Hey guys, come here with your ships. You too, Will," yells Gil from the webbed patio chair he's opened next to the car. We gather around and he says, "The aircraft carrier didn't turn over, but your battleships did. Why do you think that happened?"

We mumble to ourselves when Milt says, "Will's ship is wider than ours."

"Good one, Milt. You nailed it," which brightens up Milt.

"Will's carrier has what engineers call a low center of gravity. Every building, boat, car, or… statue, every single thing, manmade or not, has a center of gravity. It's the place where the mass, sort of like the weight of an object, is centrally located in relation to the horizontal force of gravity — like a road, an ocean or the ground. It determines the stability of an object.

"A pickup truck is fairly stable; the center of gravity is somewhere behind the lower middle of the front seat. But if you pile twenty mattresses in the back, the center of gravity will rise a lot, probably above the cab. It will be top-heavy. When you turn a corner or a wind picks up, the truck will want to fall over because the CG, as we call it, wants to be as close to gravity's pull as possible."

By now we are fully confused, but sort of get the idea. "Doug's *Missouri* is about a foot tall and six inches wide. The CG is probably about half way up the ship. In the water it wants to locate itself as close to the water as it can, so it flips over." He turns the ship on its side, points with his finger and says, "The center of gravity is still in the same place, but now it's as close to the water as it can get, so it's stable but useless."

"Dad, we could put on some pontoons like a catamaran, so it's wider."

Will says, "We could, but it wouldn't look like a battleship."

"What do you think, Milt?"

"I'm not sure. Maybe if Doug took off some of the top decks, the center would lower, and it'd be more stable." Doug hates this idea and starts to poke Milt, but his dad waves him off.

"That might work. Tim, what do you think?"

Groping for an idea, I remember seeing an article in *Popular Mechanics* about a new kind of racing yacht with a special hydrodynamic keel. "Maybe if it had a deep keel, it would lower the CG."

Gil crinkles the laugh lines around his eyes. "Well, let's do that." He picks up his tackle box and removes some wire and a six-inch length of galvanized water pipe. He flips the *Missouri* upside down, puts in a screw about a third forward of its bare hull, then another one toward the stern. He wraps off the wire at the bow, threads it through the pipe, ties it off at the back screw and turns the ship upright.

Touching the pipe he says, "We've added a lot more weight below the deck, so the center of gravity is located much lower to the deck. The *Missouri* is ready." He then gives our super battleships the same treatment and says, "Go, check them out."

We run to the water. Doug's battleship rides the water tall and true. Milt and I put in our ships at the same time, and they float perfectly with all 37 guns ready for the enemy, and, of course, Will's carrier cuts through the water. We immediately began spinning a lively narrative of our fleet standing off Nazi rockets, kamikazes, and North Korean PT boats. Our grasp of history is a bit fuzzy, but our spirit to resist tyranny makes up for it.

Gil sits in the webbed chair in his undershirt. He unwraps a cigar. Lights it up. Takes a couple drags before he opens the Thermos. He pours himself a drink and leans back to watch over us.

The Ford is parked just above the shore line between two pristine dunes facing the absolutely still waters of Half Moon Bay. As the sun sets, the surface begins to glow like hot cast glass, the dunes glimmer like enormous piles of gold dust, and we cavort up to our knees in the salty water reliving a variety of improbable naval battles simultaneously. The *Missouri* pounds Tokyo Bay, and our super-battleships fight German Dreadnoughts and Soviet cruisers. I proclaim that my ship is manned by Hungarian Freedom Fighters, even as my anti-aircraft guns shoot down dive-bombing Stukas and Mitsubishi Zeros. Will's aircraft carrier launches diverse aircraft from Navy Hellcats to F-86 Saber jets against Russian MIGs and German U-boats.

We have these model aircraft at home, we've seen the newsreels and the war movies, and we were all born a dozen years or less after World War II. The Korean War had only ended a few years before. The Suez Crisis — the French, British, Israeli invasion of Egypt, which was only 1,500 miles away from us in Dhahran — had just ended with disaster for everyone involved. We aren't quite little militarists, but all these wars are maybe too familiar to us.

Once the sun set, it was quickly dark. Gil had dug a shallow pit a few feet in front of his chair, filled it with wood scraps, added kerosene from a beat-up gallon tin, and set it off. After it has burned for a while, he says, "Hey guys, time for dinner!"

We have run out of enemies for the moment, so we pick up our undefeated ships and scramble to the pungent, crackling fire, seating ourselves around it in a half circle like Kung bushmen.

"Here's dinner. Mitzi made us tuna fish salad sandwiches." I didn't like tuna fish but perk up when Gil says, "And a cold Pepsi."

Milt likes tuna fish, so I slip him my sandwich, sip my soda, and watch Gil sitting across the fire munching his tuna fish salad. He's just finished chewing the last of his sandwich when he pauses to take a deep puff of his cigar, exhales, and says, "Do you guys know about Vikings?"

As far as we knew, they were pirates with dragonheads on their boats who attacked out of nowhere. Kirk Douglas's movie *The Vikings* hadn't been released in Dhahran yet, so we weren't well informed.

"Didn't they discover Greenland?" says Will.

"Yeah," says Doug, "and they attacked beach towns, robbed everyone, and took away slaves."

"Yeah, they had red beards and swords and fought like demons," adds Milt.

I say, "I never understood why they would burn up a perfectly good ship when the king died."

"The Viking funeral was a great tribute to a warlord. Laid to rest in his ship with his weapons, his gold, and his horses, his warriors would torch the boat and push it to sea. It was their way to send him to Valhalla – that was their word for heaven." Gil stops for a moment watching us across the fire. His face lit from below with flickering flames, he looks like a medicine man that I had seen in a cowboy movie.

"In a way it was like a big goodbye from the men who had fought at his side for years. A final salute in his honor and memory. Before... before they started fighting each other to see who'd be the next king."

Gil leans forward in his chair and slowly scans our faces, "Maybe we should have a Viking funeral."

We are silent. Burn our ships? Doug uncomfortably shifts his grip on his pride and joy, the USS Missouri. Milt and I are torn between our pine battleships, crudely crafted with great pride, and the flaming spectacle of arson at sea, when Will settles it: "Wicked! The plastic planes will look so cool when they catch fire." We agree that this is the best idea that we've ever heard.

Gil drains the silver cup and screws it back onto the Thermos. "Okay gentlemen, we have a funeral to attend to."

When we turn to the beach, we are fire blind and can't see anything but darkness. Gradually our pupils expand. The sun has set long ago, and the moon hasn't begun to rise. It would have been pitch black, but this is Saudi Arabia, and the sky is brilliant with stars. So many and so bright that the starlight casts a shadow. The air is dead calm with not the slightest breeze. Without a ripple or a swell, the surface of the bay looks as if it were poured from a giant bucket of fresh ebony paint.

Gripping our ships, we hit the beach at the same time, splashing into water up to our knees when a dazzling green light ensnares us as if we are being electrocuted in some sci-fi movie. It's phosphorescence caused by trillions of tiny marine organisms that glow brightly when disturbed. This just adds to the fun as we push our ships around and run our arms through the water to make it flash like neon.

Gil wades in up to his knees with the kerosene can and a long stick. "Okay, we'll start with oldest first. Doug, you're up."

"Oh, cool," says Doug as he splashes over to put his ship in the water. With one hand Gil pours kerosene over the USS Missouri, pours a little on the end of the stick and hands the can to Doug.

"Okay, here goes." He flips his Zippo and touches it to the stick. Once it is burning bright, he taps the flaming stick on Doug's ship, and it goes up in a whoosh. We are jumping up and down with excitement. Then Gil gives the legendary battleship a push with the stick, and it sails straight and true for about five yards trailing a wake of sparkling phosphorescence shaped like a widening V that slowly fades away.

Doug is yelling out instructions to the crew, "Fire Gun 4, Zero coming off the bow, Anti-aircraft get it. Boom, Boom, Boom, Got 'em. Watch out for the submarine…."

Milt shouts out, "Abandon ship," and Doug punches him in the arm, but even Gil laughs. Milt's super battleship is next, and once it's fully aflame Gil gives it a swift shove that cruises the ship past the Missouri as Milt starts a live sound-effects track complete with dive bombers, anti-aircraft, and heavy cannon punctuated with torpedo strikes and bomb explosions.

Will's flattop with its burning flight deck glides far out into the water. The little plastic airplanes do light up nicely, each one sending up black tendrils of burning plastic mixed with the smoke. The superstructure is burning wildly. And we are transfixed.

Earlier I had dribbled some beach mud over the deck of my ship, so when I put it in the water Gil says, "What's this?" And after a second, "Oh, I remember. Camouflage."

I'm still a bit reluctant about scorching my masterpiece, but I give him the thumbs up. He splashes his kerosene, waits a few beats, torches my boat, and pushes it into the bay. A thin, shimmering, green trail of phosphorescence follows in the wake of the warship as it coasts out to the flaming fleet.

Doug and Milt's battleships burn furiously, but the carrier is like a campfire. The whole deck is ablaze, the plastic airplanes long ago cinders. My ship is burning all right but more like a candle flame than a bonfire.

All five of us stand silently in the starlight, knee-deep in the bay. Like a mirror made of black glass, the water reflects the four burning ships exactly. It looks as if there are eight ships on fire.

A slight breeze ripples the water and stokes the flames. The aircraft carrier sends up a fiery plume as the thin plywood deck burns through and snaps in half. The two sides capsize into each other and sizzle out in the water.

Milt's super battleship is nose heavy with blockhouses and cannons so, when the stern cabin burns up, it corkscrews into the drink. The *Missouri* is still flaming near the waterline before a small wave washes over the deck to end the light.

My ship is still on fire, so I'm watching closely. The other guys are, too, but their attention is wandering because they are out of the hunt. They drift back to the beach where Doug picks up a mud ball and tosses it at Milt, but hits Will. So they run down the beach laughing and throwing mud at each other.

I'm still watching... and so is Gil, who hasn't taken his gaze off the boats since he torched the *Missouri*. After a minute he says, "It must be the camouflage, Tim."

"What?"

"The camouflage. Look! It's burning like a Coleman lantern. The mud is acting like a wick, so the kerosene isn't burning the wood as much. But it will."

"I wonder how long it will take?"

Still looking at the flaming boat, he says, "We'll see."

The battleship drifts farther into the bay, Gil stands forward on his toes like a bear. His shoulders are up as if he smells something in the air, only his eyes are moving. Scanning the horizon and then coming back to the burning hulk. Staring at it. He falls into a sort of trance, and I turn back to watch the final act.

Knowing now what I discovered some 40 years later, I have to wonder if Gil was staring into the past only a dozen years earlier, as seen from a battleship off Omaha Beach. Maybe it was his way of saying goodbye.

The flames finally devour the soft pine, and my battleship rolls over. The sea is black again. The night is quiet as we stand up to our knees in the water looking into the darkness.

Without a glance at me, Gil says, "Did you give your ship a name?"

"Yeah, the *Budapest*."

He doesn't respond for a moment and then nods, "*Budapest*?"

"It's in Hungary. It was the battleship of the Hungarian freedom fighters. I wanted them to win."

"I did, too. They fought like hell, but it just wasn't in the cards." He is kind enough to not point out that there was no Hungarian navy.

All of Half Moon Bay is before us. The glow of a rising gibbous moon in the east arrives to soften the night. Gil says, "Look up there," and points to the Milky Way.

In those days, much fewer than ten thousand people lived within ten miles of the bay. There is zero water pollution, zero air pollution, and zero light pollution, so the galaxy is as bright and clear as you could ever hope to see it.

We're looking up at the stars when Gil says, "The universe is so... so beautiful. We may not know everything about how it works. But we do know that it is beautiful." He paws me in the head and says, "Maybe that's enough. Let's go."

At the beach Gil turns as if he has just remembered something: "Tim. If you were a ship, where would your center of gravity be?"

I grab my stomach and say, "Here."

He bends over so that his already big face is much closer to mine and says, "But you are not a ship. You are a man. Your center of gravity is here," and he lightly taps his heart. He straightens up, looks directly into my eyes, pats his chest again, and softly says, "Here."

ACKNOWLEDGMENTS

For 16 years Vicci Turner has served a vital, online community of people from Pakistan to California, from Australia to Denmark who all at one time worked and lived in Aramco and loved it. Just my kind of people. I'm grateful to Vicci for publishing most of these stories on AramcoExpats.com.

Thanks to the many readers whose comments and emails have encouraged me to ramble on about various misadventures and exploits within the sleepy oil camp of Dhahran. It's a small world, but it's our world, and I don't try too hard to explain all the particulars to outsiders because you had to be there to hear the siren that every day signaled the end of the work day at five o'clock or the Ramadan cannon that announced to the faithful that it was time to eat and drink after a day of fasting.

I'm am very grateful to David Hills, a lifelong friend and extraordinary photographer, and my brilliant niece and proofreader Medora Brown who has rendered my fractured syntax and entirely random punctuation into proper sentences.

ABOUT THE AUTHOR

Born and raised in Dhahran, as an adult Tim Barger worked in Riyadh for the King Faisal Specialist Hospital and in 1977 established the Saudi Arabian Electronics Equipment Company in Jeddah for servicing video equipment, installing closed circuit systems, and distributing licensed programming to hotels and compounds.

After his return to America in 1980, he started a media company that produced technical films and videos for 20 years. In 1999 he produced his father's memoir *Out in the Blue: Letters from Arabia 1937 – 1940*. Since then he has published a dozen books about the Middle East, Saudi Arabia in particular.

His novel about love in the time of Rock and Roll, *Pamela's Song,* was released in 2012. His first collection of stories, *Arabian Son: 21 Stories*, has found a wider audience beyond Aramcons to include third-culture children who grew up in mining camps in Chile or the towns of the Canal Zone in Panama, as well as the lady who wrote from South Dakota. She didn't know much about Saudi Arabia, but she enjoyed the stories because they reminded her of a mischievous cousin she knew when she was growing up in Sioux Falls.

If you enjoyed reading CHRISTMAS in KHOBAR, you may be interested in ARABIAN SON, Tim Barger's first collection of stories. Available at Amazon in print or e-book.

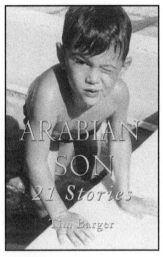

ARABIAN SON: 21 Stories
E-book: $4.95
Paperback: 142 pages ~ $14.95
ISBN: 978-098820505-5